THIRD EDITION

XML
Pocket Reference

*Simon St.Laurent
and Michael Fitzgerald*

Beijing · Cambridge · Farnham · Köln · Paris · Sebastopol · Taipei · Tokyo

XML Pocket Reference, Third Edition
by Simon St.Laurent and Michael Fitzgerald

Published by O'Reilly Media, Inc., 1005 Gravenstein Highway North,
Sebastopol, CA 95472.

O'Reilly books may be purchased for educational, business, or sales
promotional use. Online editions are also available for most titles
(*safari.oreilly.com*). For more information, contact our corporate/
institutional sales department: (800) 998-9938 or *corporate@oreilly.com*.

Editor:	Simon St.Laurent
Production Editor:	Claire Cloutier
Cover Designer:	Hanna Dyer
Interior Designer:	David Futato

Printing History:

October 1999:	First Edition.
April 2001:	Second Edition.
August 2005:	Third Edition.

0-596-10050-7
[C]

Contents

Introduction   1
   A Simple XML Document   4

XML Structures   5
   Elements   6
   Attributes   13
   Text   15
   Character, Entity, and Predefined Entity References   16
   Comments   19
   The XML Declaration   20
   Processing Instructions   22
   CDATA Sections   24
   The DOCTYPE Declaration   24
   The xml:space Attribute   26
   The xml:lang Attribute   27
   The xml:id Attribute   28
   XML Namespaces   29

Document Type Definitions   32

W3C XML Schema   47
   Creating a Simple Schema   48
   Compositors   56
   XML Schema Structure Elements   64

XML Schema Datatypes	85
XML Schema Constraining Facets	102
XML Schema Attributes for Use in Instance Documents	116

RELAX NG — **118**

Schematron — **150**
Core Elements	152
Other Elements	154

XML Specifications — **160**

Index — **163**

XML Pocket Reference

Introduction

After several years of incredible hype, XML, the Extensible Markup Language, has settled down to become a respectable part of developers' toolboxes. XML's structured, text-based format has made it easy for programming languages and environments to support it, making XML the *lingua franca* of the data exchange world. XML wasn't the first way to do this, but it was the first that successfully attained approachable simplicity while representing complex data structures.

XML provides its users with tremendous flexibility. It defines a set of hierarchical structures for containing content, but leaves the details of those structures, including their names, to the people who create XML vocabularies. XML's common structures make it possible to create parsers and other toolkits that work on any legal XML out there, while still allowing customization of the data stored in those documents. Developers can do generic processing on XML documents as well as create applications that understand particular types of XML documents.

This reference covers the core of the XML standards for representing data, including the core structures of XML 1.0 and 1.1, namespaces, and schema languages for describing XML vocabularies. It doesn't cover tools for processing XML.

In this latest edition of the book, Extensible Stylesheet Language Transformations (XSLT) has been moved to a new, well-earned location in a separate O'Reilly book—the *XSLT 1.0 Pocket Reference*—to make room here for schema information.

Conventions Used in This Book

Italic
> Used for filenames, URIs, new terms, and emphasis

Constant width
> Used for names of XML elements, attributes, etc.; code excerpts; characters; values; and other literal text

Constant width italic
> Used for text to be replaced by the user

Constant width bold
> Used for emphasis within code excerpts

XML is a greatly simplified version of SGML, the Standard Generalized Markup Language (ISO 8879:1986(E)). Any legal XML document is, in fact, a legal SGML document, but while SGML found most of its use in document-intensive operations that often required the use of its many features, XML reduced that feature set and is consequently much easier to use.

That simplicity has been rewarded with ubiquity. XML support is available for pretty much every programming language now in use, though every language seems to treat it differently.

The core of XML work, including responsibility for the key specifications for XML 1.0, XML 1.1, Namespaces in XML 1.0 and 1.1, and XML Schema, is done at the World Wide Web Consortium (W3C). For more on their operations, visit *http://www.w3.org/*. The W3C is not by any means the only organization in the business of creating XML specifications. To see a huge list of XML-based specifications and information on the and organizations and individuals creating them, visit *http://xml.coverpages.org/*. A brief list appears at the end of this book.

XML documents must be *well-formed*, or in other words, they must follow the rules of *well-formedness* laid down in the XML spec. A well-formedness error is fatal in XML processing. XML documents may also, but need not, be valid; That is, they may conform to a DTD or schema if a schema is available and if validation is performed with a validating XML processor.

Differences Between XML 1.0 and 1.1

The main differences between Versions 1.0 and 1.1 are that Version 1.1:

- Supports a later version of Unicode (4.0)
- Has a more liberal policy for characters used in names
- Adds a couple of line-end characters (NEL [#x85] and the Unicode line separator character [#x2028])
- Allows character references for control characters that are forbidden in 1.0

For details, see *http://www.w3.org/TR/xml11/#sec-xml11*.

A Simple XML Document

If you're new to XML or just need to identify a feature you haven't seen before, looking at a sample document may be helpful. The document shown in Example 1 contains a variety of XML features.

Example 1. A simple XML document

```
 1  <?xml version="1.0" encoding="UTF-8" standalone="no" ?>
 2  <?xml-stylesheet href="mine.css" type="text/css" ?>
 3  <!--This is a very simple document.-->
 4  <!DOCTYPE message SYSTEM "myMessage.dtd" >
 5  <message xmlns="http://simonstl.com/ns/examples/message"
 6           xmlns:xsi="http://www.w3.org/2001/XMLSchema-
             instance"
 7           xsi:schemaLocation="message.xsd"
 8           xml:lang="en" date="2005-10-06" >
 9    This is a message!
10  </message>
```

This document contains many common XML structures, each of which is described briefly here and in greater detail later in this book. Line 1 is an optional XML declaration that provides version and encoding information, plus a declaration that indicates whether or not the document stands alone (i.e., whether it relies on external markup declarations). Line 2 is a *processing instruction*—more precisely, an XML stylesheet processing instruction that references a local CSS stylesheet. Line 3 is a *comment* and line 4 is a *document type declaration* (or DOCTYPE declaration) that points to a *document type definition*, or DTD. A DTD contains rules for document validation. The message element start-tag, on line 5, is the root (or document) element. This element contains several attributes with varying purposes. The attribute on line 5 (xmlns) happens to be a namespace declaration, as is the attribute on line 6 (namespace declarations are not normally processed like other attributes). The xsi:schemaLocation attribute, on line 7, associates the document with an XML Schema document, also used for validation. The `xml:lang` attribute, on line 8, specifies that the English language is in use here, and the date attribute value contains an ISO 8601–formatted date. Line 9 shows the text content or character data content of the `message` element. Finally, line 10 is the end-tag for the `message` element. All of these features and more are covered in this pocket reference.

XML Structures

Everything in an XML document is text—typically Unicode text. Special characters (primarily < and >, but also &, ", and ') are used to separate the text that identifies document structures from the text contained in those structures. The text that represents the structure of the document is called *markup*, as historically it was extra information added to text documents to provide metadata, formatting, or other information. Adding this information to a document is referred to as "marking up" the document, although text and markup are usually created simultaneously now.

As each structure is discussed, applicable productions from the XML 1.0 and 1.1 specs will be listed in the order in which they appear in the specs. However, productions for Letter, BaseChar, IdeoGraphic, CombiningChar, Digit, and Extender are omitted here for the sake of brevity (refer to Appendix B in the 1.0 spec, at *http://www.w3.org/TR/REC-xml/#CharClasses*). If there are differences between the 1.0 and 1.1 productions, the line representing the production will be appended by either *1.0* or *1.1*; otherwise, the productions in both specs are the same. Productions may be repeated for the reader's convenience.

You will find references to the XML specification in this section. Any reference preceded by a section symbol (§) is a reference to the XML spec. For example, §2.1 refers to Section 2.1 of the XML 1.0 and 1.1 specifications.

Elements

Elements, which are the building blocks of XML documents, are bounded by start-tags and end-tags that may hold content, or may consist of one empty-element tag.

Productions

```
[2] Char ::= #x9 | #xA | #xD | [#x20-#xD7FF] | [#xE000-
#xFFFD] | [#x10000-#x10FFFF] 1.0
[2] Char ::= [#x1-#xD7FF] | [#xE000-#xFFFF] | [#x10000-
#x10FFFF] 1.1
[3] S ::= (#x20 | #x9 | #xD | #xA)+
[4] NameChar::= Letter | Digit | '.' | '-' | '_' | ':' |
CombiningChar | Extender 1.0
[4] NameStartChar ::= ":" | [A-Z] | "_" | [a-z] | [#xC0-
#xD6] | [#xD8-#xF6] | [#xF8-#x2FF] | [#x370-#x37D] |
[#x37F-#x1FFF] | [#x200C-#x200D] | [#x2070-#x218F] |
[#x2C00-#x2FEF] | [#x3001-#xD7FF] | [#xF900-#xFDCF] |
[#xFDF0-#xFFFD] | [#x10000-#xEFFFF] 1.1
[4a] NameChar ::= NameStartChar | "-" | "." | [0-9] | #xB7
| [#x0300-#x036F] | [#x203F-#x2040] 1.1
[5] Name::= (Letter | '_' | ':') (NameChar)* 1.0
[5] Name ::= NameStartChar (NameChar)* 1.1
[10] AttValue ::= '"' ([^<&"] | Reference)* '"' | "'"
([^<&'] | Reference)* "'"
[14] CharData ::= [^<&]* - ([^<&]* ']]>' [^<&]*)
[15] Comment ::= '<!--' ((Char - '-') | ('-' (Char - '-
')))* '-->'
[16] PI ::= '<?' PITarget (S (Char* - (Char* '?>'
Char*)))? '?>'
[17] PITarget ::= Name - (('X' | 'x') ('M' | 'm') ('L' |
'l'))
[18] CDSect ::= CDStart CData CDEnd
[19] CDStart ::= '<![CDATA['
[20] CData ::= (Char* - (Char* ']]>' Char*))
[21] CDEnd ::= ']]>'
[25] Eq ::= S? '=' S?
[39] element ::= EmptyElemTag | STag content Etag
[40] Stag ::= '<' Name (S Attribute)* S? '>'
[41] Attribute ::= Name Eq AttValue
[42] Etag ::= '</' Name S? '>'
[43] content ::= CharData? ((element | Reference | CDSect
| PI | Comment) CharData?)*
```

```
[44] EmptyElemTag ::= '<' Name (S Attribute)* S? '/>'
[66] CharRef ::= '&#' [0-9]+ ';' | '&#x' [0-9a-fA-F]+ ';'
[67] Reference ::= EntityRef | CharRef
[68] EntityRef ::= '&' Name ';'
```

Examples

```
<data>This is some data!</data>

<photo source="photos/mypic.jpg" description="photo of
  moi" />

<message xmlns="http://simonstl.com/ns/examples/message"
  xml:lang="en" date="20051006" >
  This is a message!
</message>

<date>
 <year>2005</year>
 <month>July</month>
 <day>01</day>
</date>

<mixed>This is a <italic>mixed</italic> message!</mixed>
```

Description

The most common structure in XML documents is the element. Every XML document is required to have one complete element in it, which may in turn contain other elements or attributes. (It is possible and acceptable to create documents that contain only elements and content, without using any of the other features of XML.)

Elements always have names. Element names must start with a letter, underscore, or colon (though colons are definitely discouraged) and may contain numbers and a wide range of other characters, though whitespace is prohibited because it marks the end of an element name.

Element names are case sensitive. The set of allowed characters in element names broadened from XML 1.0 to XML 1.1, shifting from rules that forbade everything not permitted to rules that allow everything not specifically excluded.

Although colons are allowed in XML element names, they should be reserved for use with qualified or prefixed names in namespaces, as most XML processors today expect colons to separate namespace prefixes from the local element name. Even if you don't know what namespaces are or don't care to use them, you should avoid using colons in your element names.

Start-tags and end-tags. Elements are identified with tags, which come in three varieties: start-tags, end-tags, and empty-element tags (described in the next section). Start-tags take the following general form: `<elementName [attributes]>`. A start-tag without attributes might look like this: `<myElement>`. Start-tags indicate the beginning of an element, which reaches its end (or "is closed") when a matching end-tag appears. End-tags look like this: `</elementName>`. Attributes may never appear in end-tags, but whitespace after the *elementName* is allowed. An end-tag matching the start-tag shown above would look like this: `</myElement>`. Because element names are case sensitive, the case of the *elementName* in the end-tag must precisely match that of the *elementName* in the start-tag, character for character, case for case.

Empty-element tags. Empty-element tags indicate both the beginning and end of an element in one construct. They look much like start-tags but include an extra forward slash (/). For example: `<elementName [attributes] />`. The empty-element tag `<myElement />` is equivalent to `<myElement></myElement>`. An empty-element tag is simply an abbreviation for a start-tag and end-tag and no content.

TIP

Just like start-tags and end-tags, empty-element tags let you include whitespace between the element name and the closing bracket, in this case `/>`. A space between the element name and the `/>` is more common in empty-element tags, probably because this practice avoids problems with older browsers and is recommended by XHTML.

Elements can contain any other XML component that may legally appear in a document except the DOCTYPE declaration and its contents. Attributes may appear in start- or empty-element tags. Elements, text, processing instructions, comments, entities, and CDATA sections may all appear in the content of an element, between the start-tag and the end-tag.

Element nesting. Everything inside an element (except attributes, which are listed in start- or empty-element tags) must nest cleanly. An element can't contain another element's start-tag without containing its end-tag as well. Also, an element can't contain the start of a comment or CDATA section without containing its end. Any structure that begins inside a given element must end inside that element. For instance, this is illegal:

```
<sentence>These are <b>bold, <i>bold italic,</b>, and
italic</i>.</sentence>
```

The b element contains the start-tag of the i element but not its end-tag, while the i element contains the end-tag for the b element but not its start-tag. An XML parser should come to a halt when it encounters the `</b>` without having encountered an `</i>` first. To fix this particular problem, you'd need to restructure the tags like this:

```
<sentence>These are <b>bold, <i>bold italic,</i></b><i>,
and italic</i>.</sentence>
```

Now the first b element cleanly contains an i element, and a new i element starts right after the b element closes. The structure is balanced; XML parsers will be able to read it easily.

TIP

If you need overlapping structures, XML probably isn't the right tool. You may want to explore LMNL (*http://lmnl.org*), an experimental form of markup that allows overlap. Alternatively, you may choose to work in XML but define ranges externally with tools such as the W3C's incomplete XPointer() scheme.

Structures and relationships. The hierarchical structure of XML elements lends itself to a lot of metaphors. Family metaphors and tree metaphors predominate, but sometimes the two get mixed. Here's a list of the most common metaphors:

Root or document

> The *root* or *document element* of any XML document is the first XML element and contains all of the other XML elements. The root element doesn't necessarily contain the entire document. Things like the XML declaration, comments, processing instructions, document type declarations, and whitespace can be left outside of it. The document's top level is sometimes called the *root node* (XPath 1.0) or the *document node* (XPath 2.0), but this is different than the root element because it contains not only the root element, but also the parts of the document outside the root element.

Parent

The *parent element* of any XML component is the element that directly contains it. The root element of an XML document has no parent element, though the document root itself is sometimes considered the parent of the root element.

Ancestor

An *ancestor element* is any element that contains a given node, even if there are other elements in between. The root element is an ancestor element of every element in an XML document.

Child

A *child element* is an element directly contained by another element. Child elements may in turn have children of their own, though the metaphor isn't usually extended to grandchildren and beyond. Comments, processing instructions, CDATA sections, and text nodes may also be considered children, though they aren't child elements.

Descendant

A *descendant element* is any element contained in another element. All elements are descendants of the root element.

Sibling

A *sibling element* is a component that shares the same parent as another component. In <a><b/><c/><d/></a>, the b, c, and d elements are all siblings of each other. b is sometimes called a *preceding sibling* of c, while d would be referred to as a *following sibling*.

Leaf

A *leaf element* is an element that contains no other elements, and a *leaf node* is any component that contains no other elements, text, or components.

These metaphors can be very useful for referring to specific elements within a document. Most of the environments for processing XML documents are organized based on these relationships.

Mixed content. Many XML applications, typically data applications, contain neatly organized fields of data like the following:

```
<sale>
 <item>
  <sku>033921238</sku>
  <quantity>2</quantity>
  <price>13.42</price>
 </item>
 ...
</sale>
```

Elements in these documents are nested in other elements but are not mixed with text. Elements contain either elements or text, but never both—unless they contain *mixed content*. Mixed content occurs when elements contain both text and elements, like:

```
<name><family>Smith</family>, <given>John</given></name>
```

or:

```
<para>Today, wonderful things happened in <place>New York
City</place>, where <person>Emperor Jeffrey</person> was
handing out flowers from his limousine.</para>
```

Mixed content is typically used for document-like applications, wherein it's occasionally important to highlight a particular *part* of a sentence or paragraph as having a particular nature. In the preceding example, it may be important for an application to identify places and people, perhaps for indexing purposes. The first example shows how to create a name element that includes a comma and keeps that comma from interfering with the structure and parts of the name.

Mixed content is easy to use in documents but can make some kinds of processing more difficult and create complications for DTDs and many flavors of schema. Elements can

contain whitespace, processing instructions, comments, and
child elements without being considered to have mixed content. Nor do CDATA sections mixed with text constitute
mixed content.

See also

§3, §3.1

Attributes

Attributes are name-value pairs that may appear in a start- or
empty-element tag.

Productions

```
[2] Char ::= #x9 | #xA | #xD | [#x20-#xD7FF] | [#xE000-
#xFFFD] | [#x10000-#x10FFFF] 1.0
[2] Char ::= [#x1-#xD7FF] | [#xE000-#xFFFD] | [#x10000-
#x10FFFF] 1.1
[3] S ::= (#x20 | #x9 | #xD | #xA)+
[4] NameChar::= Letter | Digit | '.' | '-' | '_' | ':' |
CombiningChar | Extender 1.0
[4] NameStartChar ::= ":" | [A-Z] | "_" | [a-z] | [#xC0-
#xD6] | [#xD8-#xF6] | [#xF8-#x2FF] | [#x370-#x37D] |
[#x37F-#x1FFF] | [#x200C-#x200D] | [#x2070-#x218F] |
[#x2C00-#x2FEF] | [#x3001-#xD7FF] | [#xF900-#xFDCF] |
[#xFDF0-#xFFFD] | [#x10000-#xEFFFF] 1.1[4a] NameChar ::=
NameStartChar | "-" | "." | [0-9] | #xB7 | [#x0300-#x036F]
| [#x203F-#x2040] 1.1
[5] Name::= (Letter | '_' | ':') (NameChar)* 1.0
[5] Name ::= NameStartChar (NameChar)* 1.1
[10] AttValue    ::= '"' ([^<&"] | Reference)* '"' | "'"
([^<&'] | Reference)* "'"
[25] Eq ::= S? '=' S?
[39] element ::= EmptyElemTag | STag content Etag
[40] Stag ::= '<' Name (S Attribute)* S? '>'
[41] Attribute ::= Name Eq AttValue
[44] EmptyElemTag ::= '<' Name (S Attribute)* S? '/>'
[67] Reference ::= EntityRef | CharRef
[68] EntityRef ::= '&' Name ';'
[69] PEReference ::= '%' Name ';'
```

Examples

```
<message xmlns="http://simonstl.com/ns/examples/message"
    xml:lang="en" date="20051006" >
    This is a message!
</message>

<photo source="photos/mypic.jpg" description="photo of
moi"/>
```

Description

In effect, attributes modify an element in some way. They appear as a list after the name of the element, and each attribute name in the list must be unique. All of the name-value pairs must be separated by whitespace. The name of the attribute is followed by an equals sign (=) and then by a quoted value. The quotes must be matched pairs of single or double quotes; in other words, you cannot mix single and double quotes when specifying a value for an attribute. Whitespace may appear between the name, equals sign, and quoted value. The order of attributes is not significant in XML. If an XML document relies on a DTD for validation purposes, attributes may have one of ten types: CDATA, ID, IDREF, IDREFS, ENTITY, ENTITIES, NMTOKEN, NMTOKENS, NOTATION, and enumeration. If an XML document relies on XML Schema for validation, the attributes as well as elements may be of any type offered by XML Schema datatypes. The special attributes xmlns and xmlns:prefix are *not* treated as regular attributes in normal XML processing (see the later section "XML Namespaces").

See also

§2.3, §3.1

Text

A sequence of characters, or text, makes up an XML document. Text consists of both markup and character data (element content).

Productions

```
[2] Char ::= #x9 | #xA | #xD | [#x20-#xD7FF] | [#xE000-
#xFFFD] | [#x10000-#x10FFFF] 1.0
[2] Char ::= [#x1-#xD7FF] | [#xE000-#xFFFD] | [#x10000-
#x10FFFF] 1.1
[2a] RestrictedChar ::= [#x1-#x8] | [#xB-#xC] | [#xE-#x1F]
| [#x7F-#x84] | [#x86-#x9F] 1.1
[3] S ::= (#x20 | #x9 | #xD | #xA)+
[4] NameChar::= Letter | Digit | '.' | '-' | '_' | ':' |
CombiningChar | Extender 1.0
[4] NameStartChar ::= ":" | [A-Z] | "_" | [a-z] | [#xC0-
#xD6] | [#xD8-#xF6] | [#xF8-#x2FF] | [#x370-#x37D] |
[#x37F-#x1FFF] | [#x200C-#x200D] | [#x2070-#x218F] |
[#x2C00-#x2FEF] | [#x3001-#xD7FF] | [#xF900-#xFDCF] |
[#xFDF0-#xFFFD] | [#x10000-#xEFFFF] 1.1
[4a] NameChar ::= NameStartChar | "-" | "." | [0-9] | #xB7
| [#x0300-#x036F] | [#x203F-#x2040] 1.1
[5] Name::= (Letter | '_' | ':') (NameChar)* 1.0
[5] Name ::= NameStartChar (NameChar)* 1.1
[14] CharData ::= [^<&]* - ([^<&]* ']]>' [^<&]*)
```

Examples

```
<messages>
 <msg>This element contains a message.</msg>
</messages>
```

Description

A character in XML is considered an atomic unit of text. Legal characters include the tab, the carriage return, the line feed, and the legal characters of Unicode and ISO/IEC 10646. Text classed as markup consists of element start-tags (including attributes), end-tags, empty-element tags, entity and character references, comments, CDATA section delimiters, XML declarations, text declarations, processing instructions, document type declarations, and any whitespace outside the document element.

All other text—namely, text that shows up inside XML elements—is element content and is called *character data*. Ampersands (&) and less-than signs (<) can't appear in character data, because they look like markup; instead, the predefined XML entity references & and < are used to represent these characters in character data (see the following section, "Character, Entity, and Predefined Entity References").

Whitespace consists of spaces (#x20), tabs (#x9), carriage returns (#xD), and line feeds (#xA) in XML 1.0; these can appear in elements and between markup. In addition, XML 1.1 includes next line (#x85) and line separator (#x2028) as line-end characters. These new characters, however, may *not* appear in element content. The line-end characters #xD, #xA, #x85, and #x2028 (or a sequence of two) must be normalized to line feeds #xA during parsing.

The characters allowed in names, such as element and attribute names, are restricted according to the Name productions.

See also

§2.2, §2.3, §2.4, §2.11

Character, Entity, and Predefined Entity References

Character, *entity*, and *predefined entity* references refer respectively to (1) a specific character in the ISO/IEC 10646 or Unicode character set (especially one not readily accessible through the keyboard), (2) a named entity, and (3) any one of the five predefined XML entities.

Productions

```
[4] NameChar::= Letter | Digit | '.' | '-' | '_' | ':' |
CombiningChar | Extender 1.0
[4] NameStartChar ::= ":" | [A-Z] | "_" | [a-z] | [#xC0-
#xD6] | [#xD8-#xF6] | [#xF8-#x2FF] | [#x370-#x37D] |
[#x37F-#x1FFF] | [#x200C-#x200D] | [#x2070-#x218F] |
[#x2C00-#x2FEF] | [#x3001-#xD7FF] | [#xF900-#xFDCF] |
[#xFDF0-#xFFFD] | [#x10000-#xEFFFF] 1.1
[4a] NameChar ::= NameStartChar | "-" | "." | [0-9] | #xB7
| [#x0300-#x036F] | [#x203F-#x2040] 1.1
[5] Name::= (Letter | '_' | ':') (NameChar)* 1.0
[5] Name ::= NameStartChar (NameChar)* 1.1
[66] CharRef ::= '&#' [0-9]+ ';' | '&#x' [0-9a-fA-F]+ ';'
[67] Reference ::= EntityRef | CharRef
[68] EntityRef ::= '&' Name ';'
```

Examples

```
<para>The &#182; symbol marks the beginning of a
paragraph.</para>

<para>The &#xB6; symbol marks the beginning of a
paragraph.</para>

<p>&copy; O'Reilly Media, Inc.</p>

<comparison>&quot;a &lt; b &gt; &amp; a=c&quot;
</comparison>
```

Description

In XML, character and entity references are formed by surrounding a numerical value or name with & and ;, as in ©, ©, or ©.

Character references. You can write character references in decimal or hexadecimal form, though each is written in a slightly different way. For example, to create a character reference in decimal for the pilcrow sign (¶), use ¶. In hexadecimal, use ¶ or ¶ (you can drop leading zeros and use upper- or lowercase in hex). The main difference between the two forms is the x in the hex form and the use of base-10 (decimal) versus base-16 (hexadecimal) numbering systems. (The hex B6 equals the decimal 182.)

Entity references. An entity reference refers to a named entity defined in a DTD, or an internal, predefined entity. You are likely familiar with the entity references in HTML, an application of SGML—references such as   for a non-breaking space, which is defined in the HTML entity *HTMLlat1.ent* (*http://www.w3.org/TR/html401/HTMLlat1.ent*). You can learn more about DTDs and entities in the section "Document Type Definitions," later in this book. Several predefined named entities are available in XML that readily demonstrate how to use named entities.

Predefined entities. Because XML uses <, >, &, and sometimes " and ' for markup, and because it's not always easy to enter every character Unicode supports using a standard keyboard or text editor, XML offers some alternative ways to represent these characters. For the characters used as markup, XML offers predefined, or built-in, entities, which are references you can use in place of the characters themselves. These entities, shown in Table 1, are built into every compliant XML processor.

Table 1. Predefined entities

Entity	Description
&	Ampersand (&)
'	Apostrophe or single quote (')
>	Greater-than symbol (>)
<	Less-than symbol (<)
"	Double quote (")

Of all of the predefined entities, only < and & are strictly necessary. You can use quotes (and apostrophes) in contexts where they don't confuse the parser—any place outside of attribute values—and > is only necessary due to arcane rules involving SGML's recognition of CDATA sections: the XML 1.0 and 1.1 specifications bar the sequence]]> from ever appearing in text. Always use the > entity reference if a greater-than sign has to follow]]. (It seems to be good practice to use > everywhere, but this is one case in which it's explicitly necessary.)

See also

§4.1, §4.6

Comments

XML comments contain human-readable information and are formed the same way SGML (and thus HTML) comments are formed.

Productions

```
[15] Comment ::= '<!--' ((Char - '-') | ('-' (Char - '-
')))* '-->'
```

Examples

```
<!--This is a very simple document.-->

<!--
    This comment is on
    several lines.
-->
```

Description

Comments begin with <!-- and end with -->. They can contain characters that are illegal in text (character data) such as & and <; however, they can't contain the character sequence -- or --->, and they cannot be nested. XML processors generally ignore comments but may keep track of them. You can place comments anywhere in an XML document except inside other markup, such as within tag brackets. You can also place comments inside document type declarations, where allowed. Entity references and parameter entity references (such as < or %data;) are allowed but not recognized or expanded inside comments.

See also

§2.5

The XML Declaration

Optional XML declarations provide version and encoding information, as well as information about external markup declarations.

Productions

```
[23] XMLDecl ::= '<?xml' VersionInfo EncodingDecl? SDDecl?
S? '?>'
[24] VersionInfo ::= S 'version' Eq ("'" VersionNum "'" |
'"' VersionNum '"')
[25] Eq ::= S? '=' S?
[26] VersionNum ::= '1.0' 1.0
[26] VersionNum ::= '1.1' 1.1
[32] SDDecl ::= S 'standalone' Eq (("'" ('yes' | 'no')
"'") | ('"' ('yes' | 'no') '"'))
[80] EncodingDecl ::= S 'encoding' Eq ('"' EncName '"' |
"'" EncName "'" )
[81] EncName ::= [A-Za-z] ([A-Za-z0-9._] | '-')* /*
Encoding name contains only Latin characters */
```

Examples

```
<?xml version="1.0" ?>

<?xml version="1.1" encoding="ISO-8859-1"?>

<?xml version="1.0" encoding="UTF-8" standalone="no" ?>
```

Description

The XML declaration is recommended by the XML spec but is not mandatory. The XML declaration is a human- and machine-readable flag that states several facts about the content of the document. If present, it must appear on the first line of the document. An XML declaration is not a processing instruction, although it looks like one. In general, it provides three pieces of information about a document: (1) the XML version information; (2) the character encoding used in the document; and (3) the standalone document declaration, which states whether or not the document stands alone—that is, whether or not it relies on markup declarations from an external source (a DTD).

Version information. If you use an XML declaration, it *must* include version information (as in version="1.0"). Currently, XML Version 1.0 enjoys the broadest use. However, Version 1.1 is also now available (*http://www.w3.org/TR/ xml11/*) and so is a possible value for version.

The encoding declaration. An optional encoding declaration (such as encoding="UTF-8") allows you to explicitly state the character encoding used in the document. *Character encoding* refers to the way characters are represented internally, usually by one or more 8-bit bytes, or *octets*. If no encoding declaration exists in a document's XML declaration, that XML document is required to use either UTF-8 or UTF-16 encoding. A UTF-16 document must begin with a special character called a Byte Order Mark, or BOM (the zero-width, no-break space U+FEFF; see *http://www.unicode.org/charts/PDF/UFE70.pdf*). As values for encoding, you should use names registered at Internet Assigned Numbers Authority (IANA; *http://www.iana.org/ assignments/character-sets*). In addition to UTF-8 and UTF-16, US-ASCII, ISO-8859-1, and Shift_JIS are some possible choices. If you use an encoding that is uncommon, make sure your XML processor supports the encoding; if it doesn't, you'll get an error.

The standalone document declaration. An optional standalone declaration (as in `standalone="no"`) can tell an XML processor whether or not an XML document depends on external markup declarations—that is, whether or not it relies on declarations in an external DTD. The standalone document declaration can have a value of yes or no. Don't worry too much about standalone declarations, because if you don't use external markup declarations, the standalone declaration has no meaning anyway, whether its value is yes or no (i.e., `standalone="yes"` or `standalone="no"`). On the other hand, if you use external markup declarations but do not have a standalone document declaration, the value no is assumed. Given these loopholes, there isn't much real need for standalone declarations (other than acting as a visual cue) unless your processor can convert an XML document from one that does not stand alone to one that does, which may be more efficient in a networked environment.

See also

§2.9, §4.3.3

Processing Instructions

A *processing instruction* is a structure in an XML document that contains an instruction to an application.

Productions

```
[16] PI ::= '<?' PITarget (S (Char* - (Char* '?>'
Char*)))? '?>'
[17] PITarget ::= Name - (('X' | 'x') ('M' | 'm') ('L' |
'l'))
```

Examples

```
<?xml-stylesheet href="mine.css" type="text/css" ?>

<?mso-application progid="Excel.Sheet" ?>
```

Description

Processing instructions, or PIs, can appear anywhere an element can appear (although the XML stylesheet PI must appear at the beginning, or prolog, of an XML document). Any PI must appear *after* the XML declaration, if one is present. A PI is bounded by the characters <? and ?>. The term immediately following <? is called the *target*. A target identifies the purpose or the name of the PI.

The XML stylesheet processing instruction is just one example of a common PI. Other examples include PIs you might find being used in DocBook (e.g., <?hard-pagebreak?>), Microsoft Word (<?mso-application progid="Word.Document" ?>), or Microsoft Excel (<?mso-application progid="Excel.Sheet" ?>). The purpose of the XML stylesheet PI is to associate a stylesheet with an XML document. The semantics of the XML stylesheet PI are like those of the HTML or XHTML link element. The structures href and type are called *pseudo-attributes*. The PI actually has six pseudo-attributes, but, to be brief, we'll only discuss href and type here (others are title, media, charset, and alternate). In the first example, href identifies a relative URI (Uniform Resource Identifier) for the stylesheet *mine.css*, and type defines a media type for the stylesheet, namely text/css.

See also

§2.6

XML stylesheet processing instruction spec: *http://www.w3.org/TR/xml-stylesheet*

text/css media type RFC: *http://www.ietf.org/rfc/rfc2318.txt*

CDATA Sections

CDATA sections are used to escape text that contains characters that would otherwise be recognized as markup.

Productions

```
[18] CDSect ::= CDStart CData CDEnd
[19] CDStart ::= '<![CDATA['
[20] Cdata ::= (Char* - (Char* ']]>' Char*))
[21] CDEnd ::= ']]>'
```

Examples

```
<markup><![CDATA[ < and & are characters used in markup ]]>
</markup>

<company><![CDATA[Simon & Associates]]></company>
```

Description

A CDATA section begins with the characters <![CDATA[and ends with]]>. CDATA sections in XML allow you to hide characters like < and & from an XML processor. These characters have special meaning in markup; < begins an element tag and & begins a character reference or entity reference.

When processed, the & character in the CDATA section is hidden from the processor so that it isn't interpreted as markup, as the start of an entity or character reference would be. As with comments, CDATA sections cannot be nested. A CDATA section must not contain]]>.

See also

§2.7

The DOCTYPE Declaration

A document type declaration contains internal markup declarations or points to external markup declarations that provide a grammar for validating a given document or class of documents.

Productions

```
[28] doctypedecl ::= '<!DOCTYPE' S Name (S ExternalID)? S?
('[' intSubset ']' S?)? '>'
[28a] DeclSep ::= PEReference | S
[28b] intSubset ::= (markupdecl | DeclSep)*
[29] markupdecl ::= elementdecl | AttlistDecl | EntityDecl
| NotationDecl | PI | Comment
```

Examples

```
<!DOCTYPE message SYSTEM "myMessage.dtd" >

<!DOCTYPE message SYSTEM "http://www.example.com/DTD/
myMessage.dtd" >

<!DOCTYPE html PUBLIC "-//W3C/DTD XHTML 1.0 Strict//EN"
"http://www.w3.org/TR/xhtml1/DTD/xhtml1-strict.dtd" >

<!DOCTYPE message [
  <!ELEMENT message (#PCDATA) >
  <!ATTLIST message date CDATA #REQUIRED >
]>

<!DOCTYPE message SYSTEM "myMessage.dtd" [
  <!ATTLIST message info CDATA #IMPLIED >
]>
```

Description

A document type or DOCTYPE declaration provides information to a validating XML parser about how to validate an XML document. The DOCTYPE keyword appears first; then the document, or root, element of the document being validated is identified, followed by either a SYSTEM or PUBLIC identifier.

SYSTEM indicates that the DTD will be found as indicated in the filename or URI that follows (also called a *system literal*; for example, "myMessage.dtd" or "http://www.example.com/DTD/myMessage.dtd").

PUBLIC hints that the DTD is standard, well known, and widely available—although technically, it just means that a public identifier is being used. This identifier is followed by a *public*

ID literal (e.g., "-//W3C/DTD XHTML 1.0 Strict//EN"), then by a system literal. If it is registered, a public ID literal is preceded by a + character; if it is not, by a – character. Following that are two slashes (//), and then the DTD owner is given (for example, W3C). Next comes a slash (/), followed by a description (for example, DTD XHTML 1.0 Strict), followed by another two slashes (//), and finally a language token (EN).

A document type declaration may also contain an internal subset DTD, which does not include SYSTEM or PUBLIC, but encloses DTD markup declarations in square brackets. Markup declarations define the elements, attributes, entities, and notations that may exist in a valid document of the given class.

Document type declarations that do not contain an internal subset point to an external subset; however, internal and external subsets may be used together, in essence combining the declarations of both. If both are used, the declarations in the internal subset in effect occur *before* those in the external subset. In such a case, matching attribute-list and entity declarations in an internal subset take precedence over those in an associated external subset. Element declarations for the same names appearing in both subsets are not allowed if the subsets are used together.

See also

§2.8

"Document Type Definitions," later in this book

The xml:space Attribute

The special attribute xml:space indicates that whitespace should be preserved as specified in element content.

Example

```
<message xmlns="http://simonstl.com/ns/examples/message"
         xml:space="preserve" lang="en" date="20051006" >
   THIS
        IS A
            MESSAGE!
</message>
```

Description

XML processors must always pass all characters that aren't markup through to an application. When xml:space is used on an element with a value of preserve, the whitespace in that element's content must be preserved as is by the application that processes it. The whitespace is always passed on to the processing application, but xml:space provides the application with a hint regarding how to process it. Another legal value for xml:space is default, which indicates that default whitespace processing by the application is acceptable (this is the default behavior in absence of the xml:space attribute). The attribute and its value also apply to child elements.

TIP

A validating XML processor must also report whitespace in element-only content (that is, the whitespace between tags in an element that can contain only elements, not character data).

See also

§2.10

The xml:lang Attribute

The xml:lang attribute is a special language identification attribute in XML that identifies the natural or formal language in which the content of the XML document is written.

Example

```
<message xmlns="http://simonstl.com/ns/examples/message"
         xml:lang="en" date="20051006" >
```

Description

The value en (English) is a language identifier defined by RFC 3066 and ISO 639. Other examples include two-letter language identifiers, such as de (German), fr (French), and es (Spanish); two-letter identifiers with country identification subtags, such as fr-CA (French used in Canada); and three-letter language identifiers, such as eng (English), ger or deu (German), fre or fra (French), and spa (Spanish).

See also

§2.12

RFC 3066: *http://www.ietf.org/rfc/rfc3066.txt*

ISO 639: search at *http://www.iso.ch* for the latest information

The xml:id Attribute

The xml:id attribute is a method for guaranteeing proper ID processing.

Example

```
<message xml:id="i-35867">This is a message</message>
```

Description

Under XML 1.0, an ID is a unique identifier to aid in processing. You can annotate an element uniquely with an attribute of type ID, as in id="i-35867" (IDs can't start with a number), which often assumes an associated DTD containing the attribute-list declaration <!ATTLIST message id ID #REQUIRED>. Likewise, XML Schema provides a mechanism for identifying markup as having type ID with the type="xs:ID" attribute, as with <xs:attribute name="id" type="xs:ID">. The problem is that non-validating yet conformant XML processors are not

---

required to refer to or process an external subset DTD (one that exists outside of the XML document), and a correct schema may not be available, so processing IDs can be troublesome. Implementation of the xml:id attribute is an attempt to guarantee that ID processing will be consistent and reliable, whether the XML processor being used is validating or not. The xml:id mechanism is currently a W3C candidate recommendation, and it's a development worth tracking. The upcoming specs for XPath 2.0—and hence XQuery and XSLT 2.0—also support xml:id.

See also

The xml:id spec: *http://www.w3.org/TR/xml-id/*

XML Namespaces

Namespaces provide a way to disambiguate names in XML documents, thus helping avoid a collision of names when multiple vocabularies are combined.

Examples

Default namespace declaration

```
<message xmlns="http://simonstl.com/ns/examples/message"
         xml:lang="en" date="20051006" >
   This is a message!
</message>
```

Qualified or prefixed namespace declaration

```
<msg:message xmlns:msg="http://simonstl.com/ns/examples/
message" xml:lang="en" date="20051006" >
   This is a message!
</msg:message>
```

Description

The special xmlns attribute, or xmlns with a prefix (for example, xmlns:xsl), specifies a namespace declaration.

Namespaces can be confusing because they can use any URI as a namespace name. The scheme or protocol name *http://* suggests that the URI identifies a resource that can be retrieved just like any other web resource using Hypertext Transfer Protocol. But this is not the case. The URI is considered simply a name and is not a guarantee of the location or existence of a resource. URIs are allocated locally, so you don't have to deal with a global registry in order to use them; however, the downside of this is you can't really police people who might use a domain name you own as part of their URI.

Without a prefix, the xmlns attribute and its value (such as *http://simonstl.com/ns/examples/message*) are considered a *default namespace declaration*. A default namespace declaration associates a *namespace name*—a URI—with one or more elements; however, a default namespace declaration *never* associates a namespace with attributes, even though those attributes may be used on elements within the default namespace. Attributes without a prefix are *not* considered part of any namespace (see "Qualified names or names with prefixes," later in this section). A local name together with its namespace name is called an *expanded name* and is often shown in descriptive text as {http://simonstl.com/ns/examples/message}message, though it is never represented this way in XML.

The default declaration associates the namespace name with an element and its children. A default namespace declaration applies only to the element where it is declared and to any of its child or descendent elements. A default declaration on the document element therefore applies to elements in the entire document. Again, it does not apply to attributes.

Qualified names or names with prefixes. In a prefixed declaration, the prefix (such as msg) is associated with the namespace name, thus making the name a *qualified name*. If you want to apply a namespace to an attribute, you *must* use a prefix in its name, which means any element or attribute in the document that is prefixed will be associated with that namespace, provided a matching namespace declaration is reachable. Once again, an attribute that does not have a prefix is never associated with any namespace. The only way you can associate an attribute with a namespace is with a prefix. Default namespace declarations never apply to attributes.

XML Linking Language, or XLink (*http://www.w3.org/tr/xlink/*), is implemented exclusively with qualified or prefixed attribute names; it uses no elements. The namespace is declared with `xmlns:xlink="http://www.w3.org/1999/xlink"`. (`xlink:` is the conventional prefix, but it is not required.) Qualified attribute names in XLink include `xlink:href`, `xlink:type`, `xlink:title`, and `xlink:show`, among others. (Though XLink became a W3C recommendation in 2001, it does not enjoy widespread use or popularity; hence it is not discussed further in this pocket reference.)

The xml: and xmlns: prefixes. The special namespace prefix `xml` is bound to the namespace URI *http://www.w3.org/XML/ 1998/namespace* and is used with attributes such as `xml:lang`, `xml:space`, and `xml:id`. Because it is built in, it doesn't have to be declared, but you may choose to declare it. However, you are not allowed to bind `xml` to any namespace name other than *http://www.w3.org/XML/1998/namespace*, and you can't bind any other prefix to the name *http://www.w3.org/XML/ 1998/namespace*.

`xmlns` is a special attribute and also can be used as a prefix. As the result of an erratum, the prefix `xmlns` was bound to the namespace name *http://www.w3.org/2000/xmlns/*. Unlike the prefix `xml:`, `xmlns` cannot be declared, and no other prefix may be bound to *http://www.w3.org/2000/xmlns/*.

Undeclaring namespaces with Version 1.1. A new spec was created for use only with XML 1.1 namespaces. Notably, this spec allows you to undeclare a previously declared namespace—that

is, with xmlns="" you can undeclare a default namespace declaration, and with xmlns:msg="" you can undeclare a namespace
associated with the prefix msg. In Version 1.0 of the namespaces
spec, a default namespace may be empty (as in xmlns=""), but
you cannot undeclare a namespace as you can in Version 1.1.

See also

XML namespaces 1.0 spec: *http://www.w3.org/TR/REC-xml-
names*

XML namespaces 1.0 errata: *http://www.w3.org/XML/xml-
names-19990114-errata*

XML namespaces 1.1 spec: *http://www.w3.org/TR/xml-names11*

URI RFC: *http://www.ietf.org/rfc/rfc2396.txt*

Document Type Definitions

A document type definition, or DTD, defines the structure or
content model of a valid XML instance.

Productions

```
[45] elementdecl ::= '<!ELEMENT' S Name S contentspec S? '>'
[46] contentspec ::= 'EMPTY' | 'ANY' | Mixed | children
[47] children ::= (choice | seq) ('?' | '*' | '+')?
[48] cp ::= (Name | choice | seq) ('?' | '*' | '+')?
[49] choice ::= '(' S? cp ( S? '|' S? cp )+ S? ')'
[50] seq ::= '(' S? cp ( S? ',' S? cp )* S? ')'
[51] Mixed ::= '(' S? '#PCDATA' (S? '|' S? Name)* S? ')*'
    | '(' S? '#PCDATA' S? ')'
[52] AttlistDecl ::= '<!ATTLIST' S Name AttDef* S? '>'
[53] AttDef ::= S Name S AttType S DefaultDecl
[54] AttType ::= StringType | TokenizedType |
EnumeratedType
[55] StringType ::= 'CDATA'
[56] TokenizedType ::= 'ID'| 'IDREF' | 'IDREFS' | 'ENTITY'
    | 'ENTITIES' | 'NMTOKEN' | 'NMTOKENS'
[57] EnumeratedType ::= NotationType | Enumeration
[58] NotationType ::= 'NOTATION' S '(' S? Name (S? '|' S?
Name)* S? ')'
```

```
[59] Enumeration ::= '(' S? Nmtoken (S? '|' S? Nmtoken)*
S? ')'
[60] DefaultDecl ::= '#REQUIRED' | '#IMPLIED' | (('#FIXED'
S)? AttValue)
[61] conditionalSect ::= includeSect | ignoreSect
[62] includeSect ::= '<![' S? 'INCLUDE' S? '['
extSubsetDecl ']]>'
[63] ignoreSect ::= '<![' S? 'IGNORE' S? '['
ignoreSectContents* ']]>'
[64] ignoreSectContents ::= Ignore ('<!['
ignoreSectContents ']]>' Ignore)*
[65].Ignore ::= Char* - (Char* ('<![' | ']]>') Char*)
```

Examples

```
<!ELEMENT message (#PCDATA)>
<!ATTLIST message date CDATA #REQUIRED>

<?xml version="1.0" encoding="UTF-8" ?>
<?xml-stylesheet href="mine.css" type="text/css" ?>
<!--This is a very simple document.-->
<!DOCTYPE message [
 <!ELEMENT message (#PCDATA)>
 <!ATTLIST message date CDATA #REQUIRED>
]>
<message xmlns="http://simonstl.com/ns/examples/message"
         xml:lang="eng" date="20051006" >
   This is a message!
</message>
```

Description

XML inherited the DTD from SGML. The DTD is the native, grammar-based language for validating the structure of XML documents—though markup declarations are not specified in XML syntax—and is interwoven into the XML 1.0 and 1.1 specifications. A DTD can define elements, attributes, entities, and notations, and can contain comments (just like XML comments), conditional sections, and a structure unique to DTDs called *parameter entities*. DTDs can be internal or external to an XML document, or both. These concepts are discussed in the following subsections.

External subset. The document in Example 2 references an external DTD, *order.dtd*, with a document type declaration. This external DTD is also called an *external subset*.

Example 2. external.xml

```
1  <?xml version="1.0" encoding="UTF-8" standalone="no"?>
2  <!DOCTYPE order SYSTEM "order.dtd">
3
4  <order id="TDI-983857">
5   <store>Prineville</store>
6   <product>feed-grade whole oats</product>
7   <package>sack</package>
8   <weight std="lbs.">50</weight>
9   <quantity>23</quantity>
10  <price cur="USD">
11   <high>5.99</high>
12   <regular>4.99</regular>
13   <discount>3.99</discount>
14  </price>
15  <ship>the back of Tom's pickup</ship>
16 </order>
```

The XML declaration on line 1 of Example 2 declares that *external.xml* does not stand alone. That's because on line 2, the document references the DTD *order.dtd*. The file *order.dtd* is considered an external entity and is called an *external subset*. The SYSTEM keyword on line 2 indicates that the DTD will be identified by a *system identifier*, which, for all practical purposes, is a URI for a local or remote file available over a network.

In the DTD *order.dtd* (shown in Example 3), all the valid structures found in *external.xml* are declared. The document, or root, element is order (line 3 of Example 3), which contains child elements that describe a purchase order.

Example 3. order.dtd

```
1  <?xml encoding="UTF-8"?>
2  <!-- Order DTD -->
3  <!ELEMENT order
   (store+,product,package?,weight?,quantity,price,ship*)>
4  <!-- id = part number -->
5  <!ATTLIST order id ID #REQUIRED
6    xmlns CDATA #FIXED "http://www.wyeast.net/order"
7    date CDATA #IMPLIED>
8  <!ELEMENT store (#PCDATA)>
9  <!ELEMENT product (#PCDATA)>
10 <!ELEMENT package (#PCDATA)>
11 <!ELEMENT weight (#PCDATA)>
12 <!ATTLIST weight std NMTOKEN #REQUIRED>
13 <!ELEMENT quantity (#PCDATA)>
14 <!ELEMENT price (high?,regular,discount?,total?)>
15 <!ATTLIST price cur (USD|CAD|AUD|EUR) "USD">
16 <!ELEMENT high (#PCDATA)>
17 <!ELEMENT regular (#PCDATA)>
18 <!ELEMENT discount (#PCDATA)>
19 <!ELEMENT ship (#PCDATA)>
```

The text declaration. Line 1 of Example 3 shows a text declaration (see §4.3.1). It is similar to an XML declaration except that: (1) version information (like version="1.0") is optional; (2) encoding declarations (such as encoding="UTF-8") are required; and (3) there are no standalone declarations (it never uses standalone).

Element type declarations and content models. Most of the lines in *order.dtd* contain element type declarations (see §3.2), one of several kinds of markup declarations (see §2.8) that may appear in a DTD. The simplest kinds have content models for parsed character data (#PCDATA), which means that these elements must contain only text—no element children. The elements declared on lines 3 and 14 of Example 3, order and price, have content models that include only child elements.

The +, ?, and * symbols denote occurrence constraints, meaning that the child elements may occur only a given number of times, as follows:

+   The element may occur one or more times

?   The element may occur zero or one time (that is, it's optional)

*   The element may occur zero or more times

If there is no occurrence constraint (i.e., the name is followed only by a comma for sequence or | for a choice), the element may appear once and only once. For a discussion on the choice operator (|), see "Mixed-content declarations," later in this section.

Attribute-list declarations. The DTD *order.dtd* has three attribute-list declarations—on lines 5, 12, and 15. (You can declare one or more attributes at a time, hence the phrase *attribute list*.) The first declares three attributes, id, xmlns, and date. (Although most XML processors treat namespaces specially, DTDs treat namespace declarations—e.g., xmlns—just like attributes; thus namespaces must be declared.) XML attributes declared in DTDs must have one of ten possible types: CDATA, ID, IDREF, IDREFS, ENTITY, ENTITIES, NMTOKEN, NMTOKENS, NOTATION, and enumeration (see §3.3.1 for an explanation of all the attribute types).

The attribute id on line 5 is of type ID, which must be a legal XML name and must be unique. It is also required (#REQUIRED)—that is, it must appear in any valid instance of the DTD.

On line 7, the attribute date is declared. The #IMPLIED keyword means the attribute may or may not appear in a legal instance. CDATA means that the value of date will be a string.

The std attribute for the weight element is declared on line 12. It is required (#REQUIRED) and is of type NMTOKEN. A name token is a single, atomic unit—a string with no whitespace. The attribute-list declaration on line 15 declares the cur (currency) attribute for the price element. It has an enumerated type. The default value in quotes is USD (United States dollar), with possible values USD, CAD (Canadian dollar), AUD (Australian dollar), and EUR (Euro). During validation, the processor supplies default values if no values are present in the instance.

Emulating namespace support in DTDs

DTDs do not directly support XML namespaces, but you can use a few tricks to emulate namespace support. The attribute xmlns (line 6 of Example 3) has a fixed value of http://www.wyeast.net/order. The #FIXED keyword means that the attribute must always have the provided default value. When an instance of this DTD is processed with a validating processor, it *will* contain the namespace declaration xmlns="http://www.wyeast.net/order". That is, the namespace declaration will be supplied by the processor if it is not present in the instance. If you want to use prefixed elements, you could, for example, change line 6 to read: xmlns:order CDATA #FIXED "http://www.wyeast.net/order". Then add the prefix order: to all the element declarations in the DTD; for example, <!ELEMENT store (#PCDATA)> becomes <!ELEMENT **order:store** (#PCDATA)>, and so forth. You will want to use defaulted attributes in namespace declarations only when you are certain your instances will use the default namespace name or URI.

Internal subset

You can also have a DTD that is internal to an XML document; this is called the *internal subset*. *internal.xml* is an example of an XML document that contains an internal subset (see

Example 4). The DTD is stored in the document type decla-ration, which encloses markup declarations in square brack-ets ([]).

Example 4. internal.xml

```
1  <?xml version="1.0" encoding="UTF-8" standalone="yes"?>
2  <!DOCTYPE order [
3  <!-- Order DTD -->
4  <!ELEMENT order
   (store+,product,package?,weight?,quantity,price,ship*)>
5  <!-- id = part number -->
6  <!ATTLIST order id ID #REQUIRED
7     xmlns CDATA #FIXED "http://www.wyeast.net/order"
8     date CDATA #IMPLIED>
9  <!ELEMENT store (#PCDATA)>
10 <!ELEMENT product (#PCDATA)>
11 <!ELEMENT package (#PCDATA)>
12 <!ELEMENT weight (#PCDATA)>
13 <!ATTLIST weight std NMTOKEN #REQUIRED>
14 <!ELEMENT quantity (#PCDATA)>
15 <!ELEMENT price (high?,regular,discount?,total?)>
16 <!ATTLIST price cur (USD|CAD|AUD|EUR) "USD">
17 <!ELEMENT high (#PCDATA)>
18 <!ELEMENT regular (#PCDATA)>
19 <!ELEMENT discount (#PCDATA)>
20 <!ELEMENT ship (#PCDATA)>
21 ]>
22
23 <order id="TDI-983857">
24 <store>Prineville</store>
25 <product>feed-grade whole oats</product>
26 <package>sack</package>
27 <weight std="lbs.">50</weight>
28 <quantity>23</quantity>
29 <price cur="USD">
30  <high>5.99</high>
31  <regular>4.99</regular>
32  <discount>3.99</discount>
33 </price>
34 <ship>the back of Tom's pickup</ship>
35 </order>
```

On line 1, the document *internal.xml* is declared stand-alone—that is, it does not depend on markup declarations in an external entity. Notice that there is no SYSTEM keyword or system identifier or system literal. This is because the markup declarations are enclosed in the document type declaration rather than in an external entity. The document type declaration (lines 2 through 21) contains the same declarations as *order.dtd*, and the document itself (lines 23 through 35) is the same as *external.xml*, except for the DOCTYPE. Internal subsets may not contain conditional sections (see "Conditional sections in DTDs," later in this book). Parameter entity references may not occur in markup declarations in internal subsets, though they may appear where markup declarations may occur (see "Parameter entities," later in this book).

Using internal and external subsets together

The document *both.xml*, shown in Example 5, uses both an internal subset and an external subset (*both.dtd* in Example 6). Notice how the document type declaration uses both the SYSTEM keyword and a system literal ("both.dtd"), and also encloses markup declarations in square brackets ([ ]). The advantage of this technique is that DTDs can be developed and used in a modular fashion, and documents can be validated with these modules whether they exist locally or in other locations (i.e., across the Internet).

Example 5. both.xml

```
<?xml version="1.0" encoding="UTF-8" standalone="no"?>
<!DOCTYPE order SYSTEM "both.dtd" [
<!-- Order DTD -->
<!ELEMENT order
(store+,product,package?,weight?,quantity,price,ship*)>
<!-- id = part number -->
<!ATTLIST order id ID #REQUIRED
                xmlns CDATA #FIXED "http://www.wyeast.net/
                order"
                date CDATA #IMPLIED>
```

Example 5. both.xml (continued)

```
<!ELEMENT store (#PCDATA)>
<!ELEMENT product (#PCDATA)>
<!ELEMENT package (#PCDATA)>
<!ELEMENT weight (#PCDATA)>
<!ATTLIST weight std NMTOKEN #REQUIRED>
<!ELEMENT quantity (#PCDATA)>
<!ELEMENT ship (#PCDATA)>
]>

<order id="TDI-983857">
 <store>Prineville</store>
 <product>feed-grade whole oats</product>
 <package>sack</package>
 <weight std="lbs.">50</weight>
 <quantity>23</quantity>
 <price cur="USD">
  <high>5.99</high>
  <regular>4.99</regular>
  <discount>3.99</discount>
 </price>
 <ship>the back of Tom's pickup</ship>
</order>
```

Example 6. both.dtd

```
<!ELEMENT price (high?,regular,discount?,total?)>
<!ATTLIST price cur (USD|CAD|AUD|EUR) "USD">
<!ELEMENT high (#PCDATA)>
<!ELEMENT regular (#PCDATA)>
<!ELEMENT discount (#PCDATA)>
```

If an external subset and an internal subset are used together, entity and attribute-list declarations in the internal subset will take precedence over those with the same names in the external subset (see §2.8). Element declarations with the same names may not be duplicated in both subsets, so no precedence rule applies to element declarations.

Parsed entities

Parsed entities provide a means to define replacement text that may be referenced. This is somewhat like an abbreviation that is replaced with the full text of its definition wherever a reference to it appears. Parsed entities may be internal or external. An internal parsed entity declares its replacement text inline as a literal string; an external parsed entity declares its replacement text in an external resource or file.

Following are three examples of internal parsed entities. Here are the declarations, which may appear in either an internal or external subset:

```
<!ENTITY date "Thursday, September 1, 2005">
<!ENTITY time "9:00 a.m.">
<!ENTITY nbsp " ">
```

The first two entities define simple strings. The third entity shows a common use: associating a name (nbsp) with a character reference—in this case, a non-breaking space ( ).

Now here are some similar examples of external parsed entities. These declarations, which may also appear in either internal or external subsets, refer to external files (the file extension *.ent* is commonly used for external entities but is not required):

```
<!ENTITY date SYSTEM "date.ent">
<!ENTITY time SYSTEM "time.ent">
```

Here is the content of *date.ent*:

```
<?xml encoding="UTF-8"?>Monday, September 5, 2005
```

And here is the content of *time.ent*:

```
10:00 a.m.
```

The external entity *date.ent* begins with an optional *text declaration*, which is similar to an XML declaration and is likewise recommended but not required. Version information (as in version="1.0") is not required in a text declaration as it is in an XML declaration, but the encoding declaration (such as encoding="UTF-8") *is* required here (though it is not required in an XML declaration). *time.ent* does not use a text declaration; in such cases, an encoding of UTF-8 or UTF-16 is assumed.

Here is another example of external parsed entities. Such entities are commonly used to reference the chapters of a book, as shown in Example 7.

Example 7. book.xml

```
<?xml version="1.0" encoding="UTF-8"?>
<!DOCTYPE book [
<!ELEMENT book (chapter*)>
<!ATTLIST book title CDATA #REQUIRED>
<!ELEMENT chapter (title,para+)>
<!ATTLIST chapter number CDATA #REQUIRED>
<!ELEMENT title (#PCDATA)>
<!ELEMENT para (#PCDATA)>
<!ENTITY ch01 SYSTEM "chapter01.xml">
<!ENTITY ch02 SYSTEM "chapter02.xml">
<!ENTITY ch03 SYSTEM "chapter03.xml">
<!ENTITY ch04 SYSTEM "chapter04.xml">
<!ENTITY ch05 SYSTEM "chapter05.xml">
]>
<book title="Simon's Musings">&ch01;&ch02;&ch03;&ch04;&ch05;
</book>
```

book.xml contains an internal subset with declarations that validate elements and attributes that exist both within it *and* in the external parsed entities that it references. The book element has as content a series of references to external parsed entities. When processed, these references will be expanded and replaced by the files they refer to.

External parsed entities could appear on the Web and be accessed by a declaration such as this one:

```
<!ENTITY date SYSTEM "http://simonstl.com/ents/date.ent" >
```

Also, a parsed entity could have a PUBLIC identifier:

```
<!ENTITY time PUBLIC "-//SimonWorks/External Parsed
Entities 1.2//EN" "http://simonstl.com/ents/time.ent">
```

Finally, here is an example of XML content that references the date and time entities (references to either the internal or external parsed entities cited earlier are identical):

```
<para>The next session will be held on &date; at &time;
sharp.</para>
```

When an XML processor expands these entity references, the replacement text is inserted in place of the references. Following is expanded text from the internal entities:

```
<para>The next session will be held on Thursday, September
1, 2005 at 9:00 a.m. sharp.</para>
```

Parameter entities

A *parameter entity*, or PE, is a special entity that can be used only in a DTD. These entities are not allowed in XML documents. A PE provides a way to store information and then reuse that information elsewhere in a DTD multiple times. A good example of this is the way the XHTML 1.0 strict DTD defines a set of core attributes. Here is a fragment from the DTD that defines a PE:

```
1  <!-- core attributes common to most elements
2     id         document-wide unique id
3     class      space separated list of classes
4     style      associated style info
5     title      advisory title/amplification
6  -->
7  <!ENTITY % coreattrs
8   "id        ID           #IMPLIED
9    class     CDATA        #IMPLIED
10   style     %StyleSheet; #IMPLIED
11   title     %Text;       #IMPLIED"
12   >
```

Lines 1 through 6 of this fragment contain a comment explaining the purpose for four attributes: id, class, style, and title. Starting on line 7, a parameter entity is declared. The percent sign (%) is a flag to the XML processor indicating a parameter entity. The name of the parameter entity is coreattrs. The information in double quotes makes up part of an attribute-list declaration, which is reused elsewhere in the DTD.

Whereas normal entity references begin with an ampersand (&), parameter entity references begin with a percent sign (%). Lines 10 and 11 show the parameter entity references %Stylesheet; and %Text;, which are defined elsewhere in the DTD as follows:

```
<!ENTITY % StyleSheet "CDATA">
    <!-- style sheet data -->

<!ENTITY % Text "CDATA">
    <!-- used for titles etc. -->
```

%Stylesheet; and %Text; expand to CDATA. As you can see, a parameter entity can contain a reference to another parameter entity. In fact, the attrs parameter entity in *xhtml1-strict.dtd* references coreattrs and two other parameter entities:

```
<!ENTITY % attrs "%coreattrs; %i18n; %events;">
```

attrs, in turn, is used over 60 times in the DTD, so you can see how handy parameter entities are for reusing information in a DTD. One reminder: parameter entity references may not occur inside of markup declarations in internal subset DTDs, though they may occur where markup declarations are permitted in internal subsets.

Other things that can go in a DTD

This section briefly covers several other things you can include in DTDs: comments, conditional sections, unparsed entities, and notations.

Comments in DTDs. DTDs can contain XML-style comments. For example, in Example 3 earlier, a pair of comments that are formed just as they would be in an XML document are used on lines 2 and 4. (For more details, see the "Comments" section, earlier in this book.)

Conditional sections in DTDs. Conditional sections allow you to include or exclude declarations in a DTD conditionally. This feature can help you develop a DTD while you are still trying out different content models. Look at this fragment:

```
<![INCLUDE[
<!ATTLIST price cur (USD|CAD|AUD|EUR) "USD">
]]>
<![IGNORE[
<!ATTLIST price cur (USD|EUR) "USD">
]]>
```

The structure that starts with the word INCLUDE indicates that the following declaration (which must be complete) is to be included in the DTD at validation time. The section marked IGNORE, however, is to be ignored.

Mixed-content declarations. Mixed content may contain character data optionally interspersed with child elements. The order and number of occurrences of child elements is not constrained. An example of a mixed-content declaration follows:

```
"<!ELEMENT para (#PCDATA | bold | italic)*>
```

This declaration uses the choice operator | and #PCDATA to indicate the presence of character data. It allows para elements to contain bold and/or italic child elements, mixed in with text or character data. An element name must not appear more than once in a single mixed-content declaration.

Unparsed entities and notations in DTDs. An unparsed entity is a resource upon which XML places no constraints. It can consist of a chunk of XML, non-XML text, a graphical file, a binary file, or any other electronic resource. Unparsed entities have a name that is associated with a system identifier or a public identifier. Unparsed entities are used in conjunction with notations. Notation declared in a DTD provides a name for a notation, which can allow an application to locate another helper application capable of processing data in the given notation. Notations are intended for use in entity and attribute-list declarations and in attribute specifications.

For example, in DocBook, a module of a DTD (*dbnotnx.mod*) is dedicated to notations. Here is a notation from that module that associates the name GIF89a with the public identifier -// CompuServe//NOTATION Graphics Interchange Format 89a//EN:

```
<!NOTATION GIF89a PUBLIC "-//CompuServe//NOTATION Graphics
Interchange Format 89a//EN">
```

Here is another example from the same module that uses a system identifier for the name PNG:

```
<!NOTATION PNG SYSTEM "http://www.w3.org/TR/REC-png">
```

Elsewhere, in another DTD that includes this module, you could declare several entities, like this:

```
<!ENTITY dbnotnx SYSTEM "dbnotnx.mod">
&dbnotnx;
...
<!ENTITY g001 SYSTEM "g001.gif" NDATA GIF89a>
<!ENTITY g002 SYSTEM "g002.png" NDATA PNG>
...
<!ELEMENT graphic EMPTY>
<!ATTLIST graphic img ENTITY #REQUIRED>
```

The entity declarations associate names with files and with the names from notations. The NDATA keyword indicates an unparsed entity. In one type of instance, you could refer to the entity in an attribute, like this:

```
<graphic img="g001"/>
...
<graphic img="g002"/>
```

TIP

The syntax for notations is the most awkward and forbidding of any syntax in XML, so you probably won't be surprised to learn that the use of unparsed entities is rare and that the applications that support them are even more rare. When people want to display graphics, they usually transform their XML into HTML or XHTML, where they can use the tried-and-true img tag.

See also

§2.8, §3.2, §3.3.1, §4.3.1

XHTML 1.0 strict DTD: *http://www.w3.org/TR/xhtml1/DTD/xhtml1-strict.dtd*

W3C XML Schema

XML Schema, sometimes abbreviated XSD or referred to as W3C XML Schema (WXS), is an XML vocabulary that enables you to describe other XML vocabularies so that programs can test whether a given document meets rules laid down in the schema. XML Schema is defined by a set of three W3C Recommendations:

XML Schema Part 0: Primer
> A tutorial for XML Schema that explains Parts 1 and 2 in less detail and with more examples and integration; available at *http://www.w3.org/TR/xmlschema-0/*

XML Schema Part 1: Structures
> An XML vocabulary for describing the structures of XML vocabularies; based on a mixture of markup and object-oriented design; available at *http://www.w3.org/TR/xmlschema-1/*

XML Schema Part 2: Datatypes
> A set of extensible types for describing the contents of XML elements and attributes, including things like integers, decimals, and dates; available at *http://www.w3.org/TR/xmlschema-2/*

The mechanisms for defining structures and datatypes both allow schema designers to create type systems that may be extended or restricted.

XML Schema 1.0, Second Edition, is the current version endorsed by the W3C, though work on XML Schema 1.1 has begun.

Creating a Simple Schema

While all schemas use the same core parts, there are a number of different structural alternatives and key pieces worth examining before diving into all of the parts. Examine the structure of Example 8.

Example 8. A simple XML document for definition in a schema

```
<?xml version="1.0" encoding="us-ascii"?>
<authors>
    <person id="lear">
        <name>Edward Lear</name>
        <nationality>British</nationality>
    </person>
    <person id="asimov">
        <name>Isaac Asimov</name>
        <nationality>American</nationality>
    </person>
    <person id="mysteryperson"/>
</authors>
```

This document contains an `authors` element, which itself contains multiple `person` elements. Each `person` element has an `id` attribute and may contain a `name` and a `nationality` element. For now, we'll treat all of the textual content of the elements and attributes as text. One way to define this document is in a schema whose structure mirrors the document, called a "russian doll" schema after the wooden *matrusch-kas*; see Example 9. The names of the elements being defined are boldfaced to make it easier to read.

Example 9. A "russian doll" schema describing the Example 8 document

```
<xs:schema xmlns:xs="http://www.w3.org/2001/XMLSchema" >
  <xs:element name="authors">
    <xs:complexType>
      <xs:sequence>
        <xs:element name="person" maxOccurs="unbounded">
          <xs:complexType>
            <xs:sequence minOccurs="0" >
              <xs:element name="name" type="xs:string" />
              <xs:element name="nationality" type="xs:
                string" />
            </xs:sequence>
            <xs:attribute name="id" type="xs:string"
              use="required"/>
          </xs:complexType>
        </xs:element>
      </xs:sequence>
    </xs:complexType>
  </xs:element>
</xs:schema>
```

This schema starts by defining the authors element, which will be the root element for the document, and its contents. Because the authors element contains more than simple text, it is defined as having an xs:complexType. That type contains a sequence of person elements. The parts of the declaration that pertain only to the authors element are shown here.

```
<xs:element name="authors">
  <xs:complexType>
    <xs:sequence>
      <xs:element name="person" maxOccurs="unbounded">
        ...
      </xs:element>
    </xs:sequence>
  </xs:complexType>
</xs:element>
```

The declaration of the person element contains an xs:complexType, which in turn contains an xs:sequence, specifying that in this case name and nationality elements (each of which contain only a string) may appear in the sequence at hand. The xs:complexType for the person element also contains a definition for the id attribute.

```
<xs:element name="person" maxOccurs="unbounded">
  <xs:complexType>
    <xs:sequence minOccurs="0" >
      <xs:element name="name" type="xs:string" />
      <xs:element name="nationality" type="xs:string"  />
    </xs:sequence>
    <xs:attribute name="id" type="xs:string"
      use="required"/>
  </xs:complexType>
</xs:element>
```

Because the name and nationality elements and the id attribute contain only strings, they are considered "simple" compared with the complex types of the elements that contain them. For example, a declaration such as:

```
<xs:element name="name" type="xs:string" />
```

is sufficient to say that "the name element will appear here and contain a string."

There are a few other pieces to examine in Example 9, notably the maxOccurs and minOccurs attributes on xs:element, and the use attribute on xs:attribute. These will be explored later in this book, in the "Varied document structures" section. But for now, you should know that you can write the schema from Example 9 in a more modular way, as shown in Example 10. Again, the names of elements are boldfaced.

Example 10. A more modular schema describing the Example 8 document

```
<?xml version="1.0" encoding="UTF-8"?>
<xs:schema xmlns:xs="http://www.w3.org/2001/XMLSchema" >

  <xs:element name="authors">
```

Example 10. A more modular schema describing the Example 8 document (continued)

```
    <xs:complexType>
      <xs:sequence>
        <xs:element maxOccurs="unbounded" ref="person"/>
      </xs:sequence>
    </xs:complexType>
  </xs:element>

  <xs:element name="person">
    <xs:complexType>
      <xs:sequence minOccurs="0">
        <xs:element ref="name"/>
        <xs:element ref="nationality"/>
      </xs:sequence>
      <xs:attribute ref="id" use="required"/>
    </xs:complexType>
  </xs:element>

  <xs:element name="name" type="xs:string"/>

  <xs:element name="nationality" type="xs:string"/>

  <xs:attribute name="id" type="xs:string"/>

</xs:schema>
```

Instead of nesting all the declarations into one xs:element, this version of the schema separates them into different parts. Only one new piece is used to do this—the ref attribute on xs:element and xs:attribute. Writing schemas this way is frequently simpler because it allows you to reuse elements in multiple places and because it separates information about how often an element or attribute may appear (maxOccurs, minOccurs, and use, which go with the ref) from information about an element or attribute's content (the type attribute, xs:complexType child element, and so on).

When the xs:element and xs:attribute declarations are moved out to be immediate children of the xs:schema element, they become *global* elements and attributes, accessible for use in any declaration. These elements also become possible root elements for the document. (It's generally easier, especially if you use namespaces, to keep xs:attribute declarations inside the elements or attribute groups that use them, rather than moving them out to become globals.)

While these two schemas are different, the model they define is exactly the same. For many record/field-based vocabularies, the simple structures presented in Examples 9 and 10 are more than enough to get work accomplished.

Namespaces

The only namespace declaration to appear in either Example 9 or Example 10 was the namespace declaration for XSD itself:

```
xmlns:xs="http://www.w3.org/2001/XMLSchema"
```

In this case, the schema defined a vocabulary that was not in a namespace, so there was no need to define an additional namespace. If, as is typical, your schemas define vocabularies that *are* in a namespace, you'll need to identify the namespace in the root xs:schema element. Example 11 shows a slightly modified version of Example 10, defining the vocabulary as belonging to the http://simonstl.com/ns/authors/ namespace. Changes to the schema appear in bold.

Example 11. A modification of Example 10 to support a namespace

```
<?xml version="1.0" encoding="UTF-8"?>
<xs:schema xmlns:xs="http://www.w3.org/2001/XMLSchema"
           targetNamespace="http://simonstl.com/ns/authors/"
           xmlns="http://simonstl.com/ns/authors/"
           elementFormDefault="qualified"
           attributeFormDefault="unqualified" >

  <xs:element name="authors">
    <xs:complexType>
```

Example 11. A modification of Example 10 to support a namespace (continued)

```
    <xs:sequence>
      <xs:element maxOccurs="unbounded" ref="person"/>
    </xs:sequence>
  </xs:complexType>
</xs:element>

<xs:element name="person">
  <xs:complexType>
    <xs:sequence minOccurs="0">
      <xs:element ref="name"/>
      <xs:element ref="nationality"/>
    </xs:sequence>
    <xs:attribute ref="id" use="required"/>
  </xs:complexType>
</xs:element>

<xs:element name="name" type="xs:string"/>

<xs:element name="nationality" type="xs:string"/>

<xs:attribute name="id" type="xs:string"/>

</xs:schema>
```

All of the changes in this example are at the top level of the schema. The targetNamespace attribute tells the XSD processor what namespace is being defined, and the xmlns attribute that follows declares that the default namespace should use that same namespace URI. (If you leave off the xmlns attribute, the connections between the ref attributes and their corresponding xs:element and xs:attribute declarations will break.) The elementFormDefault and attributeFormDefault attributes declare whether or not local elements and attributes will be namespace qualified by default. To match typical XML 1.0 practice, elements are qualified and attributes are not.

It's also worth noting that you don't have to define attributes used in documents for namespace declarations. XSD doesn't consider them attributes and doesn't validate them.

Named and anonymous type definitions

All of the types defined in Examples 9, 10, and 11 are anonymous. Only the xs:elements and xs:attributes have names, while the xs:complexType elements don't. Some of the declarations reference a named type, xs:string (a predefined datatype), but these schemas don't create any named types of their own. If you wanted to create named types for the complex type content of Example 11, you could further modularize it as shown in Example 12.

Example 12. A modification of Example 11 to break out complex types

```
<?xml version="1.0" encoding="UTF-8"?>
<xs:schema xmlns:xs="http://www.w3.org/2001/XMLSchema"
           targetNamespace="http://simonstl.com/ns/authors/"
           xmlns="http://simonstl.com/ns/authors/"
           elementFormDefault="qualified"
           attributeFormDefault="unqualified" >

  <xs:element name="authors" type="authorsContent" />

  <xs:complexType name="authorsContent">
    <xs:sequence>
      <xs:element maxOccurs="unbounded" ref="person"/>
    </xs:sequence>
```

```
</xs:complexType>

<xs:element name="person" type="personContent" />

<xs:complexType name="personContent">
  <xs:sequence minOccurs="0">
    <xs:element ref="name"/>
    <xs:element ref="nationality"/>
  </xs:sequence>
  <xs:attribute ref="id" use="required"/>
</xs:complexType>

<xs:element name="name" type="xs:string"/>

<xs:element name="nationality" type="xs:string"/>

<xs:attribute name="id" type="xs:string"/>

</xs:schema>
```

Instead of this definition of the authors element:

```
<xs:element name="authors">
  <xs:complexType>
    <xs:sequence>
      <xs:element maxOccurs="unbounded" ref="person"/>
    </xs:sequence>
  </xs:complexType>
</xs:element>
```

the schema now uses:

```
<xs:element name="authors" type="authorsContent" />

<xs:complexType name="authorsContent">
  <xs:sequence>
    <xs:element maxOccurs="unbounded" ref="person"/>
  </xs:sequence>
</xs:complexType>
```

The actual xs:element now looks more like its simpler cousins, which merely reference a datatype, while the xs:complexType becomes a separate component. This approach means the xs:complexType can be referenced by multiple elements that have the same content model, and it also means advanced schema developers can derive additional types from the authorsContent type to create variations. Additionally, XSLT 2.0 and XQuery will be able to reference data by its type. (If you don't have an explicit reason to create named types, it is generally easier to avoid them altogether.)

Varied document structures

While some XML documents, particularly those containing spreadsheet or database information, need to define only containers and possibly a sequence, richer documents often contain a much wider variety of possibilities. Sections may be optional or appear repeatedly, but may also be replaced with a variety of different choices. Choices may include or be included *by* sequences. XML Schema offers support for many different kinds of document structures.

Examples 9 through 12 have each used the xs:sequence element and the minOccurs and maxOccurs attributes shown here.

```
<xs:element name="person">
  <xs:complexType>
    <xs:sequence minOccurs="0">
      <xs:element ref="name" />
      <xs:element ref="nationality" />
    </xs:sequence>
    <xs:attribute ref="id" use="required"/>
  </xs:complexType>
</xs:element>
```

Compositors

The xs:sequence element is called a *compositor,* imposing order on its child xs:element particles. There are two other compositors available: xs:choice and xs:all. The xs:choice element permits one of a list of particles to appear, while xs:all requires all particles to appear but doesn't put constraints on the order in which they appear. In addition to setting rules for their particles, compositors also act as a group, and you can specify minOccurs or maxOccurs for the group as a whole. (The default value for both minOccurs and maxOccurs is 1.)

If you wanted to define a person element that included both name and nationality but weren't concerned about the order in which they appeared, you could use:

```
<xs:element name="person">
  <xs:complexType>
    <xs:all>
      <xs:element ref="name"/>
      <xs:element ref="nationality"/>
    </xs:all>
    <xs:attribute ref="id" use="required"/>
  </xs:complexType>
</xs:element>
```

TIP

Notice that the xs:attribute isn't part of the group. Attributes are part of the type, but the compositors apply only to element content.

If, on the other hand, you wanted to define a person element that could contain your choice of a name or alias, you might use:

```
<xs:element name="person">
  <xs:complexType>
    <xs:choice minOccurs="0" >
      <xs:element ref="name" />
      <xs:element ref="alias" />
    </xs:choice>
    <xs:attribute ref="id" use="required"/>
  </xs:complexType>
</xs:element>
```

The particles inside an xs:sequence or xs:choice may be xs:element, xs:sequence, xs:choice, xs:any, or xs:group elements. (xs:all may contain only xs:element.) For example, a choice might be situated between an element and sequence of choices:

```
<xs:element name="pachinko">
 <xs:complexType>
  <xs:choice>
    <xs:element name="simple" type="xs:string" />
    <xs:sequence>
      <xs:choice>
        <xs:element name="choice1" type="xs:string" />
        <xs:element name="choice2" type="xs:string" />
      </xs:choice>
      <xs:choice>
        <xs:element name="choiceA" type="xs:string" />
        <xs:element name="choiceB" type="xs:string" />
      </xs:choice>
    </xs:sequence>
  </xs:choice>
 </xs:complexType>
</xs:element>
```

In this case, the pachinko element may contain an element named simple or it may contain the sequence. The sequence requires either a choice1 or choice2 element (but not both) followed by either a choiceA or choiceB element (again, not both).

XML Schema prohibits certain combinations of compositors, requiring that schema structures always provide a deterministic path to a particular combination of elements; the processor should never have to keep two possible choices in mind while it works out which particle a particular element matches. Most simple schemas will never encounter these problems, but those that are more complex can fall afoul of them. For more details, see Chapter 7 of Eric van der Vlist's *XML Schema*.

When anything is allowed

If you aren't concerned about what goes into a particular element or particle, you can use the xs:any element for its content and xs:attribute to specify its attributes. You can limit the contents to particular namespaces using the namespace attribute and tell the schema validator to skip the contents using the processContents attribute. For example, if you want to create an extension element that permits any content in any namespace, you might declare it like this:

```
<xs:element name="extension">
  <xs:complexType>
    <xs:sequence minoccurs="0" maxOccurs="unbounded">
      <xs:any namespace="##any" processContents="skip" />
    </xs:sequence>
    <xs:anyAttribute namespace="##any"
processContents="skip" />
  </xs:complexType>
</xs:element>
```

The namespace attribute can hold a namespace URI (or URIs, separated by whitespace) as well as one of four wildcards:

##local

Only elements (or attributes when using xs:anyAttribute) that are not in any namespace may appear.

##targetNamespace

Only elements (or attributes when using xs:anyAttribute) in the schema's target namespace may appear.

##any

Elements (or attributes when using xs:anyAttribute) in any namespace may appear.

##other

Only elements (or attributes when using xs:anyAttribute) that are not in the schema's target namespace may appear.

The xs:any element must appear within an xs:sequence or xs:choice. The xs:anyAttribute may appear in xs:attributeGroup, as well as xs:complexType and related elements.

Model groups

If you have lots of declarations you'll be using frequently but you don't need to be able to extend or restrict them, you can use the xs:group element, first to define a group of declarations and then to reference them.

For example, the declaration for the person element in Example 10 looks like this:

```
<xs:element name="person">
  <xs:complexType>
    <xs:sequence minOccurs="0">
      <xs:element ref="name"/>
      <xs:element ref="nationality"/>
    </xs:sequence>
    <xs:attribute ref="id" use="required"/>
  </xs:complexType>
</xs:element>
```

If you planned to reuse this combination of name and nationality but not the id attribute, you could create a model group holding the sequence and reference it inside the xs:complexType. The new version would look like this:

```
<xs:element name="person">
  <xs:complexType>
    <xs:group ref="name-nationality" minOccurs="0" />
    <xs:attribute ref="id" use="required"/>
  </xs:complexType>
</xs:element>

<xs:group name="name-nationality">
  <xs:sequence>
    <xs:element ref="name"/>
    <xs:element ref="nationality"/>
  </xs:sequence>
</xs:group>
```

You can do the same thing to attributes if you have a group of attributes to be applied repeatedly. To create a set of attributes referring to URLs and giving MIME types of the desired content, you might create an xs:attributeGroup like this one:

```
<xs:attributeGroup name="retrievalInformation" >
  <xs:attribute name="href" type="xs:anyURI" />
  <xs:attribute name="mime-type" type="xs:string"/>
</xs:attribute>

<xs:element name="link">
   <xs:complexType>
      <xs:attributeGroup ref="retrievalInformation" />
   </xs:complexType>
</xs:element>
```

The link element can now have attributes named href and mime-type.

The xs:group element may contain any compositor (such as xs:sequence, xs:choice, or xs:all) and its contents. Meanwhile, xs:attributeGroup is limited to containing xs:attribute, xs:attributeGroup, or xs:anyAttribute. If you need to put both elements and attributes in a single group, use xs:complexType instead.

Empty content, mixed content, and default values

XML Schema can support two additional types of content and, in some cases, can supply content to documents. The simplest of these cases is the creation of an element (like br in HTML) that must always be empty. The easiest way to do this is to use an xs:complexType element that doesn't reference any elements, like this:

```
<xs:element name="br">
  <xs:complexType>
  </xs:complexType>
</xs:element>
```

If you want to add attributes, they can be placed in the xs: complexType element without changing the emptiness of the br element.

Another common case is that of *mixed content,* where text and elements appear on the same level of a document. A classic example is a paragraph that contains bold, italic, and underlined text. In simple HTML, it might look like this:

```
<p>This is <b>bold</b>, this is <i>italic</i>, and this is
<u>underline</u>.</p>
```

To make this work, you need to create a definition of the p element that contains an xs:complexType element whose mixed attribute is set to true:

```
<xs:element name="p">
   <xs:complexType mixed="true">
      <xs:choice minOccurs="0" maxOccurs="unbounded">
        <xs:element name="b" type="xs:string" />
        <xs:element name="i" type="xs:string" />
        <xs:element name="u" type="xs:string" />
      </xs:choice>
   </xs:complexType>
</xs:element>
```

The choice will permit as many b, i, and u elements as necessary, while mixed="true" will permit text to be mingled with any of them.

If instead of these fancy features you just want to create a definition that provides a default value to an element or attribute if none is provided, you can use the default attribute on simple element or attribute declarations. To create an element called name whose value defaults to Winky if the element is present but empty, you would write:

```
<xs:element name="name" default="Winky" />
```

To create an attribute named flavor whose value defaults to vanilla, you would write:

```
<xs:attribute name="flavor" default="vanilla" />
```

Unlike the element, the default value will be applied only if the attribute is absent. You can also fix a value to an attribute or element. If you wanted to insist that the flavor must always be vanilla, you could instead use:

```
<xs:attribute name="flavor" fixed="vanilla" />
```

The flavor attribute's value will default to vanilla if the attribute isn't present in the document, and an error will be reported if a document contains a flavor attribute with any other value.

Annotations

XML Schema also provides support for annotations. Every single element in XML Schema permits an xs:annotation element as its first child (except xs:annotation itself, that is). The xs:annotation element may contain any number of xs:documentation and xs:appinfo elements, and the content models for both of these are wide open.

The xs:appinfo element is intended for machine-readable content, while the xs:documentation element is intended for human-readable content. Both elements accept a source attribute that points to a URI, and xs:documentation also accepts an xml:lang attribute that specifies the human language in which the documentation appears. xs:documentation in particular is an opportunity for you to provide additional information in your schemas. For example, to document the flavor attribute's peculiar status, a careful schema writer might modify its definition, as shown here:

```
<xs:attribute name="flavor" fixed="vanilla">
  <xs:annotation>
    <xs:documentation xml:lang="en-US">
      While many people like multiple flavors of ice
      cream, the manager of this project insists that
      everyone must have vanilla, and accepts no questions
      on the matter.
    </xs:documentation>
  </xs:annotation>
</xs:attribute>
```

You can also use HTML, DocBook, or the XML vocabulary of your choice within xs:documentation and then use this additional schema information with other programs or stylesheets to create more formal documentation.

XML Schema Structure Elements

These elements form the body of any XML schema, defining the document structure for documents valid against the schema. Meanwhile the datatypes, described in the later section "XML Schema Datatypes," define the contents that fit into that structure.

xs:all

Attributes

maxOccurs
    Present, but fixed at 1

minOccurs
    Either 0 or 1

Contents

    xs:annotation?, xs:element*

The xs:all element is used to create groups of elements that can appear in any order within their parent. Like the xs:all element itself, the xs:element declarations contained by xs:all have another restriction placed on them: all of their minOccurs and maxOccurs attributes must be set to 0 or 1.

xs:annotation

Attributes

None, except id.

Contents

    (xs:appinfo | xs:documentation)*

The xs:annotation element provides easy extensibility for any XML Schema declaration. The xs:annotation element may be the first child of any XML Schema element (except for xs:annotation itself), and its two child elements can contain any well-formed XML, allowing schema designers to add their own custom information to schema declarations as they see fit.

xs:any

Attributes

maxOccurs
> Any non-negative integer or unbounded.

minOccurs
> Any non-negative integer.

namespace
> One of ##any, ##other, or a list of URIs used to limit the namespaces of the elements that may appear here. The URI list may include the special value ##targetNamespace, meaning the schema's target namespace, and ##local, to indicate that elements without a namespace may appear. ##any is the default, allowing elements in any namespace. ##other allows elements in any namespace *except* the schema's target namespace.

processContents
> One of lax, skip, or strict. If strict (the default), all elements appearing here must either be declared in the schema or have a valid xsi:type attribute and must conform to those declarations. If skip, elements don't need to be declared; if they are declared, they don't need to be valid. If lax, elements don't need to be declared, but if they are declared or have an xsi:type attribute, they have to be valid according to that declaration.

Contents

```
xs:annotation?
```

The xs:any element is used to specify contents very loosely. At its loosest, an xs:any element of the following form:

```
<xs:any minOccurs="0" maxOccurs="unbounded"
namespace="##any" processContents="skip" />
```

is almost as flexible as the ANY element type in DTDs, allowing any kind of well-formed element (though not textual) content. The attributes may be used to provide more control over the contents, limiting them by quantity (minOccurs, maxOccurs), namespace (namespace), or the kind of schema processing they should receive (processContents).

xs:anyAttribute

Attributes

namespace
> One of ##any, ##other, or a list of URIs used to limit the namespaces of the attributes that may appear here. The URI list may include the special value ##targetNamespace, meaning the schema's target namespace, and ##local, to indicate that attributes without a namespace may appear. ##any is the default, allowing attributes in any namespace. ##other allows attributes in any namespace *except* the schema's target namespace.

processContents
> One of lax, skip, or strict. If strict (the default), all attributes appearing here must be declared in the schema and must conform to those declarations. If skip, attributes don't need to be declared; if they are declared, they don't need to be valid. If lax, attributes don't need to be declared, but if they are declared, they have to be valid according to that declaration.

Contents

```
xs:annotation?
```

The xs:anyAttribute element is used to specify attribute contents very loosely. The attributes may be used to provide more control

---

over which attributes are allowed to appear, limiting them by namespace (namespace) or the kind of schema processing they should receive (processContents). Like xs:attribute, this element may only appear inside an xs:complexType element.

xs:appInfo

Attributes

source
> A URI pointing to additional information

Contents

Any well-formed XML or nothing.

The xs:appInfo element is used within xs:annotation elements to provide machine-readable information—typically for information beyond that which is supported by XML Schema itself, such as additional Schematron rules. This information may be referenced by the source attribute or included directly in the xs:appInfo element's contents. There are no restrictions on the content of the xs:appInfo element, provided it is well formed.

Unlike nearly every other element in XML Schema, the xs:appInfo element cannot have an id attribute.

xs:attribute

Attributes

default
> A value for the attribute that should be reported in cases where instance documents don't explicitly include the attribute. (An xs:attribute element may have either a default attribute or a fixed attribute, but not both.)

fixed
> A value for the attribute that cannot be changed. Documents may not provide a different value for the attribute, and this value is provided if the documents don't explicitly include the attribute. (An xs:attribute element may have either a default attribute or a fixed attribute, but not both.)

form

> Takes the values qualified and unqualified. If qualified, the attribute must be used—with a prefix—in the schema's target namespace. If unqualified, the attribute must be used without a namespace. (form provides an opportunity to override the attributeFormDefault attribute of the xs:schema element.) This only works on local attribute declarations.

name

> The local name of the attribute. Note that this is *not* the qualified name; the namespace for the attribute is determined by the value of the form attribute if name is used. (An xs:attribute element may have either a name attribute or a ref attribute, but not both. An xs:attribute element that uses name must also provide a type attribute to complete the definition of the attribute; otherwise, it defaults to xs:anySimpleType.)

ref

> The namespace-qualified name of the attribute to be included by reference to a declaration at the top level of the schema. (An xs:attribute element may have either a name attribute or a ref attribute, but not both.)

type

> The namespace-qualified type of the attribute's contents. (An xs:attribute element that uses name must also provide a type attribute or an xs:simpleType child element to complete the definition of the attribute; otherwise, it defaults to xs:anySimpleType.)

use

> One of three values: optional (the default), prohibited, or required. optional and required are fairly self-explanatory, but prohibited is used to exclude attributes when performing derivation by restriction.

Contents

> xs:annotation?, xs:simpleType?

The xs:attribute element may appear only inside an xs:complexType or xs:attributeGroup element. It may either define an attribute, using name, or reference an attribute, using ref. Either the type attribute or an xs:simpleType child element may define the allowed contents of the attribute being defined.

xs:attributeGroup

Attributes

name

> The unqualified name of the attribute group that is being defined. (Attribute groups take the target namespace of the schema.) xs:attributeGroup elements with the name attribute may appear only as children of xs:schema and xs:redefine elements.

ref

> The unqualified name of the attribute group that is being referenced. (Attribute groups take the target namespace of the schema.) xs:attributeGroup elements with the ref attribute may be included in xs:attributeGroup, xs:complexType, xs:extension, and xs:restriction elements.

Contents

```
xs:annotation?, ( (xs:attribute | xs:attributeGroup)*,
                  xs:anyAttribute?) )
```

The xs:attributeGroup element is used to define and reference collections of attributes. Uses of xs:attributeGroup that define the groups must have a name attribute and may include xs:annotation, xs:attribute, xs:attributeGroup, and xs:anyAttribute child elements. Uses of xs:attributeGroup that reference previously defined attribute groups must have a ref attribute and are typically empty, though they may contain an xs:annotation child element.

xs:choice

Attributes

maxOccurs

> Any non-negative integer or unbounded. (Defaults to 1, but cannot be specified when xs:choice appears inside an xs:group element.)

minOccurs

> Any non-negative integer. (Defaults to 1, but cannot be specified when xs:choice appears inside an xs:group element.)

Contents

```
xs:annotation?, ( xs:element | xs:group | xs:choice |
                  xs:sequence | xs:any )*
```

The xs:choice element specifies that any one of the definitions included inside it (xs:element, xs:group, xs:choice, xs:sequence, or xs:any) may appear. When the xs:choice element is used outside an xs:group element, the maxOccurs and minOccurs attributes may set the number of times this choice can happen. The default is 1, but it can be set higher—even to unbounded–allowing the creation of elements that contain an arbitrary number of mixed elements.

xs:complexContent

Attributes

mixed
> Can be set to true when mixed content is allowed; false when mixed content is prohibited

Contents

```
xs:annotation?, ( xs:restriction | xs:extension )
```

The xs:complexContent element is used when deriving new complex types by extending or restricting existing complex types. It can contain an optional xs:annotation element followed by either an xs:restriction or an xs:extension element. The use of the mixed attribute depends on the type being extended or restricted. If the content of xs:complexContent is an xs:extension, it must match the mixed attribute of the type being extended.

xs:complexType

Attributes

abstract
> Set to false (the default) when the type can appear in a document; true when it can be used only as a base for deriving other types.

block
> Used to determine whether subtypes of the type can appear where the type is specified. If set to extension, then extensions

of this type may not appear where it is used. If set to
restriction, then restrictions of this type may not appear
where it is used. If set to #all, then neither extensions nor
restrictions of this type may appear where it is used.

final

Used to determine whether or not subtypes of the type can be
defined in the schema. If set to extension, then extensions of
this type may not be defined. If set to restriction, then
restrictions of this type may not be defined. If set to #all, then
neither extensions nor restrictions may be defined.

mixed

Can be set to true when mixed content (text interspersed
among the child elements) is allowed; false when mixed
content is prohibited. (The default is false.)

name

A name for the type, not a namespace-qualified name.

Contents

```
xs:annotation?, ( xs:simpleContent | xs:complexContent |
                   ( (xs:group | xs:all | xs:choice | xs:
                   sequence )?,
                   ( (xs:attribute | xs:attributeGroup)*,
                   xs:anyAttribute? ) ) )
```

The xs:complexType element is a key component for most schemas,
allowing the creation of types that can be restricted or extended, as
well as simpler things such as elements with attributes. The
attributes define rules for the type, while the contents of the xs:
complexType element define the contents of the type. The attributes
may be influenced by declarations earlier in the schema. The final
attribute will default to the value of the finalDefault attribute on
the root xs:schema element, while the block attribute will default to
the value of the blockDefault attribute on the root xs:schema
element.

The contents may include xs:annotation followed by a content definition: xs:simpleContent, xs:complexContent, or possibly a series of
xs:group, xs:all, xs:choice, and xs:sequence elements. Once the
content has been defined, attributes may be defined, using xs:
attribute, xs:attributeGroup, and xs:anyAttribute.

xs:documentation

Attributes

source
> A URI pointing to additional information

xml:lang
> A language identifier specifying which language is used by the documentation

Contents

Any well-formed XML, or nothing.

The xs:documentation element is used within xs:annotation elements to provide human-readable information—typically documentation about the components being defined in the schema. That information may be referenced by the source attribute or included directly in the xs:documentation element's contents. There are no restrictions on the content of the xs:documentation element provided it is well formed.

Unlike nearly every other element in XML Schema, the xs:document element cannot have an id attribute.

xs:element

Attributes

abstract
> Set to false (the default) when the element can appear in a document; true when this element can be replaced only with a member of its substitution group.

block
> Normally, you can use the xsi:type attribute to indicate that a particular instance of the element has a type that is a subtype of the type it's declared to have in the schema. You can also substitute an element with a member of its substitution group. If block is set to #all, then you can't do either of these things. If block is set to extension, then the instance element's type can't be an extension of the declared type. If block includes restriction, then the instance element's type

can't be a restriction of the declared type. If block includes substitution, then the element can't be substituted with a member of the substitution group.

final

Used to determine whether other elements can use this element as the head of their substitution group. If set to extension, then members of this element's substitution group can't have types that are extensions of this element's type. If set to #all, then members of this element's substitution group must have the same type as this element.

form

Takes the values qualified and unqualified. If qualified, the element must be used—with a prefix—in the schema's target namespace. If unqualified, the element must be used without a namespace. (form provides an opportunity to override the elementFormDefault attribute of the xs:schema element.) form works only on local declarations.

maxOccurs

Any non-negative integer or unbounded. (Defaults to 1, but cannot be specified when xs:choice appears inside an xs: group element.) Defines the maximum number of times this element can be repeated in a valid document. Global element declarations—those that are direct children of the xs:schema root element—cannot use maxOccurs. When xs:element is contained in an xs:all element, the value of maxOccurs may only be 0 or 1.

minOccurs

Any non-negative integer. (Defaults to 1, but cannot be specified when xs:choice appears inside an xs:group element.) Defines the minimum number of times this element can be repeated in a valid document. Global element declarations—those that are direct children of the xs:schema root element—cannot use minOccurs. When xs:element is contained in an xs: all element, the value of minOccurs may only be 0 or 1.

name

A name for the element, not a namespace-qualified name. When name is used, the ref attribute cannot be used.

nillable
> Can be true or false, and indicates whether or not instances of this element can use the xsi:nil attribute (when the element is empty) to indicate a nil value as opposed to an empty value.

ref
> The qualified name of the element being referenced. When ref is used, the name attribute cannot be used.

substitutionGroup
> The namespace-qualified name of the substitution group to which this element belongs.

type
> The namespace-qualified type of the element's contents. An xs:element element that uses name must provide either a type attribute or type information in its child elements to complete the definition of the attribute. Otherwise, it defaults to xs:anyType.

Contents

```
xs:annotation?, ( (xs:simpleType | xs:complexType)?,
                  (xs:unique | xs:key | xs:keyref)* )
```

xs:element is used to declare elements. If the xs:element appears as a child of the root xs:schema element, it is a global declaration, meaning it's available for use in other declarations and is a possible root element for instance documents conforming to the schema. xs:element may appear either as a declaration of a new element (using the name and type attributes or type information in its content) or, using the ref attribute, as a reference to a previously defined element.

xs:extension

Attributes

base
> The namespace-qualified name of the type being extended

Contents

```
xs:annotation?, ( (xs:group | xs:all | xs:choice | xs:
                 sequence)?,
                ((xs:attribute | xs:attributeGroup)*,
                 xs:anyAttribute? ))
```

xs:extension is used to define extensions to the type specified in base. It can appear in xs:simpleContent and xs:complexContent, but when it appears in xs:simpleContent, it can specify only additional attributes, not element content. When additional elements are specified, they must appear *after* the contents specified in the original base definition.

xs:field

Attributes

xpath
> An XPath expression used by the xs:unique, xs:key, or xs:keyRef element containing the xs:field

Contents

xs:annotation?

xs:field is used within xs:unique, xs:key, or xs:keyRef elements and stores an XPath location path. These expressions use a very simplified subset of XPath, permitting only abbreviated syntax for the child (/), descendent-or-self (//), and attribute axes to be used. (In place of explicit element names, the * expression may be used to match any name, and the prefix:* expression to match any name in a given namespace.) Multiple location paths may be stored in the xpath attribute, each separated by a vertical bar.

xs:group

Attributes

maxOccurs
> Any non-negative integer or unbounded.

minOccurs
> Any non-negative integer.

name
> The unqualified name of the group being defined. (Groups get their namespace from that of the schema.) xs:group elements with the name attribute may appear only as children of xs:schema and xs:redefine elements.

ref
> The unqualified name of the attribute group being referenced. (Groups get their namespace from that of the schema.) xs:group elements with the ref attribute may be included in xs:choice, xs:complexType, xs:extension, xs:group, xs:restriction, and xs:sequence elements.

Contents

```
xs:annotation?, (xs:group | xs:all | xs:choice | xs:
                 sequence)
```

xs:group with the name attribute lets you define content model fragments that can then be used elsewhere in the schema, including by xs:group elements with the ref attribute. All of these groups are global to the schema.

xs:import

Attributes

namespace
> The namespace URI of the content defined in the imported schema

schemaLocation
> A URI identifying where to find the schema to be imported

Contents

```
xs:annotation?
```

xs:import lets your schema reference schemas for namespaces other than the one your schema uses, effectively incorporating their declarations so that your content can include their content. It can also be used to include schemas that use no namespace whatsoever.

xs:include

Attributes

id
>   A unique ID value (optional)

schemaLocation
>   A URI identifying where to find the schema to be imported

Contents

>   xs:annotation?

xs:include is used when you want to break your large schema into several smaller and potentially reusable parts. All the declarations in the included files must use the target namespace of the schema doing the inclusion. (If they don't identify a target namespace, they will be assigned the namespace of the schema doing the inclusion, which allows the creation of highly-flexible "chameleon" schema components.) Inclusions are allowed to be circular: Schema A can include schema B, which can in turn include schema A. You cannot change the definitions of included schemas using this element; to do that, use xs:redefine.

xs:key

Attributes

name
>   A name for the key (not namespace qualified, as it uses the namespace of the schema)

Contents

>   xs:annotation?, (xs:selector, xs:field+)

xs:key lets you state that parts of a document must have specific values unique across the set of parts for the document to be valid. An xs:key element uses the XPath value in an xs:selector element to identify where the key applies, and the xs:field element to specifically identify which part of the document must be both present and unique among those values.

xs:key elements may appear only as children of xs:element. The xs:selector XPaths are calculated from the element in which the key is defined, while the xs:field XPaths are calculated from the selector. The name attribute is used for identification with xs:keyref. Also, xs:key behaves exactly like xs:unique, except that xs:unique does not require the values it identifies to be present.

xs:keyref

Attributes

id
: A unique ID value (optional)

name
: A name for the key reference

refer
: The qualified name of the xs:key or xs:unique referenced by the key reference

Contents

    xs:annotation?, (xs:selector, xs:field+)

xs:keyref allows the creation of constraints that compare values across document components. It does this by specifying that the values of the fields for the elements specified by selector must match the contents of the key identified by refer.

xs:list

Attributes

itemType
: A qualified name of the type contained within the list

Contents

    xs:annotation?, xs:simpleType?

xs:list is used to specify that a whitespace-separated list of values that conforms to a specific type should be used as content. This is called *derivation by list* and is only possible in the context of an xs:simpleType element. The type to which values conform may be identified through either the itemType attribute or a child xs:simpleType element, but not both.

xs:notation

Attributes

name
> A name for the notation

public
> A public identifier used for the notation, like those used in DTD NOTATION declarations

system
> A URI used as a system identifier for the notation, like those used in DTD NOTATION declarations

Contents

> xs:annotation?

xs:notation recreates the NOTATION functionality of XML 1.0 DTDs, but adds namespace qualification to their names. xs:notation is used in conjunction with the xs:NOTATION type, which can contain an enumerated list of types that have been defined using xs:notation.

xs:redefine

Attributes

schemaLocation
> A URI identifying where the processor should find the schema to be included

Contents

> xs:annotation?

xs:redefine behaves exactly like xs:include, importing definitions from schema modules in the same namespace (or in no namespace). The only difference is that when xs:redefine is used, definitions imported from those modules may be overridden through new definitions. (The exceptions to this are xs:element, xs:attribute, and xs:notation, which you cannot redefine.)

xs:restriction

Attributes

base
> The type whose content is being modified to create a new type

Contents

```
xs:annotation?,
(xs:simpleType?, (xs:enumeration | xs:fractionDigits |
                  xs:maxExclusive | xs:maxInclusive |
                  xs:minExclusive | xs:minInclusive |
                  xs:pattern | xs:pattern)* ) |
( (xs:group | xs:all | xs:choice | xs:sequence )?,
( (xs:attribute | xs:attributeGroup)*,
  xs:anyAttribute? ) )
)
```

xs:restriction allows you to create derived types in which the content model is the same as, or reduced from, the base type. Any type created using xs:restriction must be capable of being validated against the type from which it is derived. The base type may be identified with either the base attribute or the xs:simpleType child element, but not both. The content constraints for simple types must be defined using the vocabulary for simple types, while those for complex types must be defined using the vocabulary for complex types.

xs:schema

Attributes

attributeFormDefault
> A schema-wide setting for whether the form attribute on xs:attribute elements should default to qualified or unqualified (the default).

blockDefault
> A schema-wide setting for whether the block attribute on xs:element and xs:complexType elements should default to #all or some combination of extension, restriction, or substitution.

elementFormDefault
> A schema-wide setting for whether the form attribute on xs:element elements should default to qualified or unqualified (the default).

finalDefault
> A schema-wide setting for whether the final attribute on xs:element and xs:complexType elements should default to #all, extension, or restriction.

targetNamespace
> A URI that is the namespace used by all components defined in this schema. If no target namespace is specified, the elements and attributes will be in no namespace unless, perhaps, they are included by xs:include, which may assign a different namespace to unqualified components.

version
> The version of the schema this particular document represents.

xml:lang
> The human language used to write the schema.

Contents

```
((xs:include | xs:import | xs:redefine | xs:annotation)*,
 ((xs:simpleType | xs:complexType | xs:group |
  xs:attributeGroup) | xs:element | xs:attribute |
  xs:notation), xs:annotation* )*
```

xs:schema is the container element in which all other schema components must be placed. Its attributes set the target namespace used throughout the schema as well as a number of defaults for other declarations.

xs:selector

Attributes

xpath

> An XPath location path used by the xs:unique, xs:key, or xs:keyRef element containing the xs:selector

xs:selector is used within xs:unique, xs:key, or xs:keyRef elements and stores an XPath location path. These expressions use a very simplified subset of XPath, permitting only abbreviated syntax for the child axis to be used. In place of explicit element names, the * expression may be used to match any name, and the prefix:* expression to match any name in a given namespace. // may be used for any descendant, but only at the *beginning* of the XPath. No predicates or attributes may be used. Multiple location paths may be stored in the xpath attribute, each separated by a vertical bar.

xs:sequence

Attributes

maxOccurs

> Any non-negative integer or unbounded

minOccurs

> Any non-negative integer

Contents

```
xs:annotation?, ( xs:element | xs:group | xs:choice |
              xs:sequence | xs:any )*
```

The xs:sequence element specifies that the definitions included inside it (xs:element, xs:group, xs:choice, xs:sequence, or xs:any) must appear in the order they are listed. When the xs:sequence element is used outside an xs:group element, the maxOccurs and minOccurs attributes may set the number of times this choice can happen. The default is 1, but it can be set higher—even to unbounded—allowing the creation of elements that contain an arbitrary number of repetitions of a particular sequence of elements.

xs:simpleContent

Attributes

id
> A unique ID value (optional)

Contents

> xs:annotation?, (xs:extension | xs:restriction)

xs:simpleContent is used within xs:complexType elements when defining a complex type with simple content (text content plus attributes), when either extending an existing simple type (adding attributes) or restricting an existing complex type with simple content (removing attributes or restricting the simple content). All of the type definition takes place within the child xs:extension or xs:restriction elements.

xs:simpleType

Attributes

final
> Used to determine whether or not subtypes of the type can be defined in the schema. If set to list, then this type may not be extended by list. If set to union, then this type may not be extended by union. If set to restriction, then restrictions of this type may not be defined. If set to #all, then neither lists, unions, nor restrictions may be defined.

name
> A name for the type, not a namespace-qualified name.

Contents

> xs:annotation?, (xs:restriction | xs:list | xs:union)

xs:simpleType elements may be used directly in xs:schema or xs:redefine elements, in which case they define types identified with their name attribute. Or they may be used in xs:attribute, xs:element, xs:list, xs:restriction, or xs:union elements, in which case they define anonymous types that are used strictly within those contexts.

The nature of the type is defined by restriction, list, or union, but must be based on a simple type (either predefined by XML Schema or user-defined in the schema).

xs:union

Attributes

memberTypes
> A whitespace-separated list of the base types that may appear in the type

Contents

```
xs:annotation?,  xs:simpleType*
```

xs:union permits the creation of simple types that may take more than one kind of data—both an xs:boolean and an xs:byte, for example. The list of those types may appear in the memberTypes attribute and/or in child xs:simpleType elements. If both are used, the list of types will include both sets of possibilities.

xs:unique

Attributes

name
> A name for the key (not namespace-qualified)

Contents

```
xs:annotation?, (xs:selector, xs:field+)
```

xs:unique lets you state that parts of a document must have values unique across the set of parts for the document to be valid. An xs:unique element uses the XPath value in an xs:selector element to identify where the constraint applies and the xs:field element to specifically identify which part of the document must be unique among those values. (Values may also be missing.)

xs:unique elements may appear only as children of xs:element. The xs:selector XPaths are calculated from the element in which the key is defined, while the xs:field XPaths are calculated from the selector. The name attribute is used for identification with xs:keyref. Also, xs:unique behaves exactly like xs:key, except that xs:key requires the values it identifies to be present.

XML Schema Datatypes

XML Schema provides 19 primitive types, 25 derived types, and 1 unusable base type. Most of these types fall into a few families, representing strings, numbers, lists, dates and times, and a few other pieces such as encoded binary values.

xs:anySimpleType

Facets

Effectively none (users cannot derive from anySimpleType)

xs:anySimpleType is used only in the schema for XML Schema itself and is the theoretical ur-type from which all XML Schema types derive.

xs:anyURI

Facets

xs:enumeration, xs:length, xs:maxLength, xs:minLength, xs:pattern, xs:whiteSpace

The xs:anyURI type is meant to hold the URIs (including URLs) normally contained by the XLink (and also the HTML) href attribute. Its use isn't limited to this, however, and developers may apply it to any situation in which using URIs is appropriate.

While the xs:anyURI type is designed to store URIs, it doesn't do any special, URI-specific processing to them. xs:anyURI doesn't include any mechanisms for making relative URIs absolute or for escaping or unescaping characters as required by RFC 2396 or 2732 when using URIs. Schema processors don't check to find out if anything is present at the target of the URI. All of this functionality, if needed, must be provided by the application after schema processing is complete.

Sample acceptable values: http://example.com/, #example, mailto:
example@example.com, urn:oid:1.3.6.1.4.1.6320, /my/monkey/index.
htm?species=Capuchin

xs:base64binary

Facets

xs:enumeration, xs:length, xs:maxLength, xs:minLength, xs:
pattern, xs:whiteSpace

The xs:base64binary type is designed to contain information represented using the Base64 algorithm described in RFC 2045 (*http://ietf.*
org/rfc/2045.txt). Base64 encoding allows applications to encode
binary data as ASCII text and retrieve it again after transmission. The
only characters allowed in Base64-encoded data are the letters A–Z
and a–z, the numbers 0–9, and the symbols plus (+) and slash (/).
The encoding uses 4 bytes for every three of these characters. The
data is represented in 76-character lines (because of its origins as part
of the MIME mail rules) separated by line feeds. The equals sign (=)
is used to pad lines if necessary.

TIP

The Base64 algorithm has been separated from RFC 2045
into a separate specification, RFC 3548 (*http://ietf.org/rfc/*
3548.txt). While that's a more convenient place to locate
details of the algorithm, the XML Schema specification
still normatively references RFC 2045.

While Base64 encoding is hardly an efficient means of trans-
porting information, it is somewhat more efficient than the other
type XML Schema provides for this task, xs:hexBinary.

xs:boolean

Facets

xs:pattern, xs:whiteSpace

The xs:boolean type offers only two choices for its value: true
(represented by true or 1) or false (represented by false or 0).

---

xs:byte

Facets

xs:enumeration, xs:fractionDigits, xs:maxExclusive, xs:maxInclusive, xs:minExclusive, xs:minInclusive, xs:pattern, xs:totalDigits, xs:whiteSpace

The xs:byte type stores integer values between −128 and 127. An optional leading plus or minus sign is permitted, but decimal points are not. Legal values include -128, -94, 0, 97, and +127.

xs:date

Facets

xs:enumeration, xs:maxExclusive, xs:maxInclusive, xs:minExclusive, xs:minInclusive, xs:pattern, xs:whiteSpace

The xs:date type stores individual Gregorian calendar dates in the format *CCYY-MM-DD*, where *CC* is two or more digits for the century, *YY* is the year (00–99), *MM* is the month (01–12), and *DD* is the day (01–31). For years before 1, a negative sign may appear before the century. Acceptable dates include 1999-11-25, -0044-03-15, and 2020-01-01.

A time zone relative to Coordinated Universal Time, also known as Greenwich Time or UTC, may also be added. If there is a time zone, the format is *±hh:mm*, wherein a plus or minus sign is followed by a two-digit value for hours, then a colon, and then a two-digit value for minutes. You can also use Z in place of the time zone, indicating UTC. Valid dates with a time zone include 1999-11-25+05:00, -0044-03-15-10:30, and 2020-01-01Z.

xs:dateTime

Facets

xs:enumeration, xs:maxExclusive, xs:maxInclusive, xs:minExclusive, xs:minInclusive, xs:pattern, xs:whiteSpace

The xs:dateTime type combines Gregorian calendar dates with times. Its contents appear in the format *CCYY-MM-DDThh:mm:ss*, where *CC* is the century, *YY* is the year (00–99), *MM* is the month

(01–12), *DD* is the day (01–31), *hh* is the hour (00–23), *mm* is the minute (00–59), and *ss* is the second (00–59, plus an optional decimal part). For years before 1, a negative sign may appear before the century. Acceptable xs:dateTime values include 1999-11-25T04:03:20, -0044-03-15T12:00:00, and 2020-01-01T18:47:49.

A time zone relative to Coordinated Universal Time, also known as Greenwich Time or UTC, may also be added. If there is a time zone, the format is ±hh:mm, wherein a plus or minus sign is followed by a two-digit value for hours, then a colon, and then a two-digit value for minutes. You can also use Z in place of the time zone, indicating UTC. Valid date/time combinations with a time zone include 1999-11-25T04:03:20+05:00, -0044-03-15T12:00:00-10:30, and 2020-01-01T18:47:49Z.

xs:decimal

Facets

> xs:enumeration, xs:fractionDigits, xs:maxExclusive, xs:maxInclusive, xs:minExclusive, xs:minInclusive, xs:pattern, xs:totalDigits, xs:whiteSpace

The xs:decimal type represents a base-10 number, including any number of fractional digits to the right of the decimal point. Values may include the digits 0–9 (and only those digits, not other Unicode digits), a leading plus or minus sign, and a single decimal point. xs:decimal does not support scientific notation or values representing infinity. (For those purposes you should use xs:double or xs:float.) Acceptable values include -20, +25.1, 0.2, 3.1415926535897932384626433832795, 0, -0, -0., and +.0.

xs:double

Facets

> xs:enumeration, xs:maxExclusive, xs:maxInclusive, xs:minExclusive, xs:minInclusive, xs:pattern, xs:whiteSpace

The xs:double type represents a double-precision 64-bit IEEE 754 floating-point number. In addition to the digits 0–9 (and only those digits, not other Unicode digits), a leading plus or minus sign, and a single decimal point, xs:double also accepts scientific notation and the values INF (infinity), -INF (negative infinity), and NaN (not a number). If scientific notation is used, the mantissa may be a decimal but the exponent must be an integer. No preceding plus sign may be used on the exponent, but a preceding minus sign is acceptable. An E or an e separates the mantissa and the exponent. Legal values include 3.14159265358, -2.32E90, 1.7E12, 1.7E-12, 0, and -0.

xs:duration

Facets

> xs:enumeration, xs:maxExclusive, xs:maxInclusive, xs:minExclusive, xs:minInclusive, xs:pattern, xs:whiteSpace

The xs:duration datatype is used to represent a period of time. Because periods of time may range from seconds to centuries, it uses a very flexible notation. A duration that includes a year, month, day, hour, minute, and seconds is written as PnYnMnDTnHnMnS, with a possible leading minus sign to indicate negative durations. The number preceding Y is the number of years, the number preceding the first M is months, and the number preceding the D is days. The T separator marks the start of time in the duration; the number preceding H is hours, the number preceding M is minutes, and the number preceding S is seconds and may include a decimal part. The P is always necessary, and the T is necessary if the duration uses units smaller than days. Thus, P2Y is two years. P2M is two months, and PT2M is two minutes. Seven years, four months, six days, thirteen hours, twenty minutes, and four seconds could be written as P7Y4M6DT13H20M4S. Unlike the date and time types, no leading zeros are required.

Comparing durations is difficult, but as long as durations use only year and month or day, hour, minute, and second, it is possible to reliably compare them.

xs:ENTITIES

Facets

xs:enumeration, xs:length, xs:maxLength, xs:minLength, xs:
whiteSpace

The xs:ENTITIES datatype is provided for compatibility with XML 1.0 DTDs. Its value should be a whitespace-separated list of unparsed entity names. To maintain compatibility with DTDs, this type should be used only for attributes. (Schemas can't define unparsed entities, so this type must be used in concert with a DTD.)

xs:ENTITY

Facets

xs:enumeration, xs:length, xs:maxLength, xs:minLength, xs:
pattern, xs:whiteSpace

The xs:ENTITY datatype is provided for compatibility with XML 1.0 DTDs. Its value should be an unparsed entity name. To maintain compatibility with DTDs, this type should be used only for attributes. (Schemas can't define unparsed entities, so this type must be used in concert with a DTD.)

xs:float

Facets

xs:enumeration, xs:maxExclusive, xs:maxInclusive, xs:
minExclusive, xs:minInclusive, xs:pattern, xs:whiteSpace

The xs:float type represents a single-precision 32-bit IEEE 754 floating-point number. In addition to the digits 0–9 (and only those digits, not other Unicode digits), a leading plus or minus sign, and a single decimal point, xs:double also accepts scientific notation and the values INF (infinity), -INF (negative infinity), and NaN (not a number). If scientific notation is used, the mantissa may be a decimal but the exponent must be an integer. No preceding plus sign may be used on the exponent, but a preceding minus sign is acceptable. An E or an e separates the mantissa and the exponent. Legal values include 3.14159265358, -2.32E90, 1.7E12, 1.7E-12, 0, and -0.

xs:gDay

Facets

```
xs:enumeration,  xs:maxExclusive,  xs:maxInclusive,  xs:
minExclusive, xs:minInclusive, xs:pattern, xs:whiteSpace
```

The xs:gDay type stores a day of the month in the format ---*DD*, where *DD* is the day (01–31). Acceptable values include ---25, ---15, and ---01.

A time zone relative to Coordinated Universal Time, also known as Greenwich Time or UTC, may also be added. If there is a time zone, the format is ±*hh*:*mm*, wherein a plus or minus sign is followed by a two-digit value for hours, then a colon, and then a two-digit value for minutes. You can also use Z in place of the time zone, indicating UTC. Valid xs:gDay values with a time zone include ---25+05:00, ---15-10:30, and ---01Z.

xs:gMonth

Facets

```
xs:enumeration,  xs:maxExclusive,  xs:maxInclusive,  xs:
minExclusive, xs:minInclusive, xs:pattern, xs:whiteSpace
```

The xs:gMonth type stores a month (identified by number) in the format --*MM*, where *MM* is the month (01–12). Acceptable values include --02, --12, and --01.

A time zone relative to Coordinated Universal Time, also known as Greenwich Time or UTC, may also be added. If there is a time zone, the format is ±*hh*:*mm*, wherein a plus or minus sign in followed by a two-digit value for hours, then a colon, and then a two-digit value for minutes. You can also use Z in place of the time zone, indicating UTC. Valid xs:gMonth values with a time zone include --02+05:00, --12-10:30, and --01Z.

xs:gMonthDay

Facets

xs:enumeration, xs:maxExclusive, xs:maxInclusive, xs:
minExclusive, xs:minInclusive, xs:pattern, xs:whiteSpace

The xs:gMonthDay type stores a day/month combination in the
format --MM-DD, where MM is the month (01–12) and DD is the day
(01–31). Acceptable values include --02-27, --12-25, and --01-04.

A time zone relative to Coordinated Universal Time, also known
as Greenwich Time or UTC, may also be added. If there is a time
zone, the format is ±hh:mm, wherein a plus or minus sign is
followed by a two-digit value for hours, then a colon, and then a
two-digit value for minutes. You can also use Z in place of the time
zone, indicating UTC. Valid xs:gMonthDay values with a time zone
include --02-27+05:00, --12-25-10:30, and --01-04Z.

xs:gYear

Facets

xs:enumeration, xs:maxExclusive, xs:maxInclusive, xs:
minExclusive, xs:minInclusive, xs:pattern, xs:whiteSpace

The xs:gYear type stores a year in the format CCYY, where CC is the
century and YY is the year (00–99). The overall year must include
at least four digits and may have a preceding negative sign.
Acceptable values include 1970, -0044, and 0801.

A time zone relative to Coordinated Universal Time, also known
as Greenwich Time or UTC, may also be added. If there is a time
zone, the format is ±hh:mm, wherein a plus or minus sign is
followed by a two-digit value for hours, then a colon, and then a
two-digit value for minutes. You can also use Z in place of the time
zone, indicating UTC. Valid xs:gYear values with a time zone
include 1970+05:00, 0044-10:30, and 0801Z.

xs:gYearMonth

Facets

xs:enumeration, xs:maxExclusive, xs:maxInclusive, xs:minExclusive, xs:minInclusive, xs:pattern, xs:whiteSpace

The xs:gYearMonth type stores a year/month combination in the format *CCYY-MM*, where *CC* is the century, *YY* is the year (00–99), and *MM* is the month (01–12). The overall year must include at least four digits and may have a preceding negative sign. Acceptable year/month combinations include 1970-11, 0044-03, and 0801-04.

A time zone relative to Coordinated Universal Time, also known as Greenwich Time or UTC, may also be added. If there is a time zone, the format is ±*hh*:*mm*, wherein a plus or minus sign is followed by a two-digit value for hours, then a colon, and then a two-digit value for minutes. You can also use Z in place of the time zone, indicating UTC. Valid xs:gYearMonth values with a time zone include 1970-11+05:00, 0044-03-10:30, and 0801-04Z.

xs:hexBinary

Facets

xs:enumeration, xs:length, xs:maxLength, xs:minLength, xs:pattern, xs:whiteSpace

The xs:hexBinary type is designed to contain binary information encoded as a set of hexadecimal values. The xs:hexBinary values are lists of representations of bytes, each one represented as a two-digit hexadecimal number, so the only characters that may appear in xs:hexBinary values are the numbers 0–9 and the letters A–F and a–f.

xs:ID

Facets

xs:enumeration, xs:length, xs:maxLength, xs:minLength, xs:pattern, xs:whiteSpace

The xs:ID type provides compatibility with the ID attribute type from XML 1.0 DTDs. Like those IDs, the contents of the xs:ID type must start with a letter and contain letters, digits, underscores, or colons, and the value must be unique within the document. (If you need more sophisticated tests of uniqueness, use the xs:key, xs:keyref, and xs:unique structures.)

xs:IDREF

Facets

xs:enumeration, xs:length, xs:maxLength, xs:minLength, xs:pattern, xs:whiteSpace

The xs:ID type provides compatibility with the IDREF attribute type from XML 1.0 DTDs. Like those IDREFs, the contents of the xs:IDREF type must start with a letter and contain letters, digits, underscores, or colons, and the value must match an xs:ID value elsewhere in the document.

xs:IDREFS

Facets

xs:enumeration, xs:length, xs:maxLength, xs:minLength, xs:whiteSpace

The xs:ID type provides compatibility with the IDREFS attribute type from XML 1.0 DTDs. Like that IDREFS type, the contents of the xs:IDREFS type must be a whitespace-separated list of values, each of which starts with a letter and contains letters, digits, underscores, or colons, and each of which must match an xs:ID value elsewhere in the document.

xs:int

Facets

xs:enumeration, xs:fractionDigits, xs:maxExclusive, xs:maxInclusive, xs:minExclusive, xs:minInclusive, xs:pattern, xs:totalDigits, xs:whiteSpace

The xs:int type stores 4-byte integer values between −2147483648 and 2147483647. An optional leading plus or minus sign is permitted, but decimal points are not. Legal values include -2142203700, -1294, 94, 0, 97, and +2147483647.

xs:integer

Facets

```
xs:enumeration, xs:fractionDigits, xs:maxExclusive, xs:
maxInclusive, xs:minExclusive, xs:minInclusive, xs:pattern,
xs:totalDigits, xs:whiteSpace
```

The xs:integer type represents a base-10 number without any decimal points or fractional digits. Values may include the digits 0–9 (and only those digits, not other Unicode digits) and a leading plus or minus sign. No decimal point may appear. Acceptable values include 3.14159265358979323846264338332795, -20, +25, 02, 0, -0, and +0.

xs:language

Facets

```
xs:enumeration, xs:length, xs:maxLength, xs:minLength, xs:
pattern, xs:whiteSpace
```

The xs:language type contains an RFC 1766 language code that corresponds to the acceptable values for the xml:lang attribute. Like xml:lang, the schema validator doesn't test whether or not the value corresponds to a real language. That task is left to the application.

xs:long

Facets

```
xs:enumeration, xs:fractionDigits, xs:maxExclusive, xs:
maxInclusive, xs:minExclusive, xs:minInclusive, xs:pattern,
xs:totalDigits, xs:whiteSpace
```

The xs:long type stores 8-byte integer values between the numbers −9223372036854775808 and 9223372036854775807. An optional leading plus or minus sign is permitted, but decimal points are not. Legal values include -22337203685477580, -3492294, 904, 0, 439562, and +9223372036854775806.

xs:Name

Facets

xs:enumeration, xs:length, xs:maxLength, xs:minLength, xs:
pattern, xs:whiteSpace

The xs:Name type contains character strings that are legal XML 1.0
names, starting with a letter and otherwise consisting of letters,
digits, ideographic characters, underscores, hyphens, periods, and
colons. (XML 1.1 supports a wider range of characters in names,
but XML Schema 1.0 supports the XML 1.0 rules.) Legal values
include h1223, myName, my_Name:12, silliness, money-owed, and
this.idea.

xs:NCName

Facets

xs:enumeration, xs:length, xs:maxLength, xs:minLength, xs:
pattern, xs:whiteSpace

The xs:NCName type contains character strings that are legal but non-
colonized XML 1.0 names, starting with a letter and otherwise
consisting of letters, digits, ideographic characters, underscores,
hyphens, and periods. The colon is prohibited. (XML 1.1 supports
a wider range of characters in names, but XML Schema 1.0 only
supports the XML 1.0 rules.) Legal values include h1223, myName, my_
Name12, silliness, money-owed, and this.idea.

xs:negativeInteger

Facets

xs:enumeration, xs:fractionDigits, xs:maxExclusive, xs:
maxInclusive, xs:minExclusive, xs:minInclusive, xs:pattern,
xs:totalDigits, xs:whiteSpace

The xs:negativeInteger type represents a negative base-10
number without any decimal points or fractional digits. Values
may include the digits 0–9 (and only those digits, not other

Unicode digits) and must include a leading minus sign. No decimal point may appear, and the value must be less than zero. Acceptable values include -7932384626433832795, -212320, -20, and -1.

xs:NMTOKEN

Facets

xs:enumeration, xs:length, xs:maxLength, xs:minLength, xs:pattern, xs:whiteSpace

The xs:NMTOKEN type corresponds to the XML 1.0 DTDs NMTOKEN attribute type. Its values may contain character strings that are legal XML 1.0 name tokens, consisting of letters, digits, ideographic characters, underscores, hyphens, periods, and colons. (XML 1.1 supports a wider range of characters in names, but XML Schema 1.0 supports the XML 1.0 rules.) Legal values include h1223, 3412_32, my_Name:12, silliness, money-owed, and this.idea.

xs:NMTOKENS

Facets

xs:enumeration, xs:length, xs:maxLength, xs:minLength, xs:whiteSpace

The xs:NMTOKENS type corresponds to the XML 1.0 DTDs attribute type NMTOKENS. Its value is a whitespace-separated list of xs:NMTOKEN values, which may contain character strings that are legal XML 1.0 name tokens, consisting of letters, digits, ideographic characters, underscores, hyphens, periods, and colons. (XML 1.1 supports a wider range of characters in names, but XML Schema 1.0 only supports the XML 1.0 rules.)

xs:nonNegativeInteger

Facets

> xs:enumeration, xs:fractionDigits, xs:maxExclusive, xs:
> maxInclusive, xs:minExclusive, xs:minInclusive, xs:pattern,
> xs:totalDigits, xs:whiteSpace

The xs:nonNegativeInteger type represents a positive (or zero)
base-10 number without any decimal points or fractional digits.
Values may include the digits 0–9 (and only those digits, not other
Unicode digits) and, optionally, a leading plus sign. No decimal
point may appear, and the value must be zero or more. Acceptable values include 793234643383, 212320, 1, and 0.

xs:nonPositiveInteger

Facets

> xs:enumeration, xs:fractionDigits, xs:maxExclusive, xs:
> maxInclusive, xs:minExclusive, xs:minInclusive, xs:pattern,
> xs:totalDigits, xs:whiteSpace

The xs:nonPositiveInteger type represents a negative (or zero)
base-10 number without any decimal points or fractional digits.
Values may include the digits 0–9 (and only those digits, not other
Unicode digits) and must include a leading minus sign. No
decimal point may appear, and the value must be zero or less.
Acceptable values include -793234643383, -212320, -1, and 0.

xs:normalizedString

Facets

> xs:enumeration, xs:length, xs:maxLength, xs:minLength, xs:
> pattern, xs:whiteSpace

The xs:normalizedString type is just like xs:string except that
the xs:whiteSpace facet is fixed to replace. This means that ordi-
nary spaces replace all the tabs, line feeds, and carriage returns.

xs:NOTATION

Facets

xs:enumeration, xs:length, xs:maxLength, xs:minLength, xs:pattern, xs:whiteSpace

The xs:NOTATION datatype is part of a mechanism comparable to but incompatible with NOTATION in XML 1.0 DTDs. Its value should be a namespace-qualified notation name used elsewhere in an xs:notation declaration.

xs:positiveInteger

Facets

xs:enumeration, xs:fractionDigits, xs:maxExclusive, xs:maxInclusive, xs:minExclusive, xs:minInclusive, xs:pattern, xs:totalDigits, xs:whiteSpace

The xs:positiveInteger type represents a positive base-10 number without any decimal points or fractional digits. Values may include the digits 0–9 (and only those digits, not other Unicode digits) and, optionally, a leading plus sign. No decimal point may appear, and the value must be greater than zero. Acceptable values include 7932846233832795, 212320, 20, and 1.

xs:QName

Facets

xs:enumeration, xs:length, xs:maxLength, xs:minLength, xs:pattern, xs:whiteSpace

The xs:QName type is designed to hold namespace-qualified names as defined in Namespaces in XML. It uses the same set of characters as xs:Name, but its value (which may or may not contain a prefix and a colon) is treated as if it were an element name in the current context of the document where it appears; effectively, the default namespace declaration is used if no prefix is included. The schema processor will report both the namespace URI and the local name to the receiving application.

xs:short

Facets

xs:enumeration, xs:fractionDigits, xs:maxExclusive, xs:maxInclusive, xs:minExclusive, xs:minInclusive, xs:pattern, xs:totalDigits, xs:whiteSpace

The xs:short type stores 2-byte integer values between −32768 and 32767. An optional leading plus or minus sign is permitted, but decimal points are not. Legal values include -32700, -1294, 94, 0, 97, and +12700.

xs:string

Facets

xs:enumeration, xs:length, xs:maxLength, xs:minLength, xs:pattern, xs:whiteSpace

The xs:string type is one of the most basic in XML Schema and is a common foundation for derived types. The xs:string type can contain any legal XML characters, though quotes and the apostrophe, as well as <, >, and & may need to be escaped to avoid breaking the well-formedness of the document.

xs:time

Facets

xs:enumeration, xs:maxExclusive, xs:maxInclusive, xs:minExclusive, xs:minInclusive, xs:pattern, xs:whiteSpace

The xs:time type specifies a time of day. Its contents appear in the format *hh:mm:ss*, where *hh* is the hour (00–23), *mm* is the minute (00–59) and *ss* is the second (00–59, plus a possible decimal part). Acceptable times include 04:03:20, 12:00:00, and 18:47:49.

A time zone relative to Coordinated Universal Time, also known as Greenwich Time or UTC, may also be added. If there is a time zone, the format is ±hh:mm, wherein a plus or minus sign is followed by a two-digit value for hours, then a colon, and then a two-digit value for minutes. You can also use Z in place of the time zone, indicating UTC. Valid times with a time zone include 04:03: 20+05:00, 12:00:00-10:30, and 18:47:49Z.

xs:token

Facets

xs:enumeration, xs:length, xs:maxLength, xs:minLength, xs: pattern, xs:whiteSpace

The xs:normalizedString type is just like xs:string except that with this type, all the tabs, line feeds, and carriage returns are replaced with single spaces, and leading and trailing spaces are trimmed.

xs:unsignedByte

Facets

xs:enumeration, xs:fractionDigits, xs:maxExclusive, xs: maxInclusive, xs:minExclusive, xs:minInclusive, xs:pattern, xs:totalDigits, xs:whiteSpace

The xs:unsignedByte type stores integer values between 0 and 255. An optional leading plus sign is permitted, but decimal points are not. Legal values include 255, 12, 0, 97, and +127.

xs:unsignedInt

Facets

xs:enumeration, xs:fractionDigits, xs:maxExclusive, xs: maxInclusive, xs:minExclusive, xs:minInclusive, xs:pattern, xs:totalDigits, xs:whiteSpace

The xs:unsignedInt type stores integer values between 0 and 4294967295. An optional leading plus sign is permitted, but decimal points are not. Legal values include 42921132, 12, 0, 97, and +0020221.

xs:unsignedLong

Facets

> xs:enumeration, xs:fractionDigits, xs:maxExclusive, xs:maxInclusive, xs:minExclusive, xs:minInclusive, xs:pattern, xs:totalDigits, xs:whiteSpace

The xs:unsignedLong type stores integer values between 0 and 18446744073709551615. An optional leading plus sign is permitted, but decimal points are not. Legal values include 18446744073709551615, 12, 0, 97, and +002022232121.

xs:unsignedShort

Facets

> xs:enumeration, xs:fractionDigits, xs:maxExclusive, xs:maxInclusive, xs:minExclusive, xs:minInclusive, xs:pattern, xs:totalDigits, xs:whiteSpace

The xs:unsignedShort type stores integer values between 0 and 65535. An optional leading plus sign is permitted, but decimal points are not. Legal values include 65534, 12231, 0, 97, and +12470.

XML Schema Constraining Facets

The XML Schema Part 2: Datatypes specification defines both *fundamental facets* and *constraining facets*. Fundamental facets (equal, ordered, bounded, cardinality, and numeric) are built into the definitions of the predefined datatypes and aren't available for you to use in creating your own schemas. Constraining facets, on the other hand, allow you to specify more exactly the values or kinds of values may be stored in your schema components. Applying these facets in xs:restriction elements allows you to create more precise types than those that come built into XML Schema itself. Many of these facets apply only to particular types— for instance, xs:fractionDigits wouldn't make much sense applied to strings.

All facet elements may contain xs:annotation child elements and have attributes outside the XML Schema namespace. They also share the fixed and id attributes. When the fixed attribute is set to true, the given facet cannot be modified during later restriction. The id attribute is useful if you're creating schemas automatically and need guaranteed unique identifiers on every component.

Also, some facets cannot be applied simultaneously with others. If you need to set both, you'll need to use two separate xs:restriction elements.

xs:enumeration

Allows you to specify a list of values as the only acceptable values for a given type

Applies to

All datatypes except xs:boolean

Attributes

value

> Any simple type containing values consistent with the datatype for which they are being enumerated

Operation

Unlike the other facets, the enumeration element is used repeatedly within an xs:restriction element to specify allowed values. For example, to specify a type that contains the pigment primary colors red, blue, and yellow, you might write:

```
<xs:simpleType name="pigmentPrimaries">
  <xs:restriction base= "xs:token">
    <xs:enumeration value="red" />
    <xs:enumeration value="blue" />
    <xs:enumeration value="yellow" />
  </xs:restriction>
</xs:simpleType>
```

If someone confused his light primaries with his pigment primaries and tried to enter green, the validator would reject that value.

This facet cannot be fixed. Types derived from an enumerated type must be defined as subsets of the enumerated possibilities of the original type.

xs:fractionDigits

Allows you to specify the number of significant digits to the right of the decimal separator

Applies to

`xs:decimal`

Attributes

`fixed`
    An `xs:boolean`; true or false, defaulting to false

`value`
    An `xs:nonNegativeInteger`

Operation

The number in `value` specifies the number of significant digits allowed after the decimal point. Despite the presence of other numeric types with fractional values, `xs:fractionDigits` is only available for use with `xs:decimal`.

xs:length

Allows you to specify the precise length (in characters, bytes, or list items) of a given value

Applies to

`xs:anyURI`, `xs:base64binary`, `xs:ENTITIES`, `xs:ENTITY`, `xs:hexBinary`, `xs:ID`, `xs:IDREF`, `xs:IDREFS`, `xs:language`, `xs:Name`, `xs:NCName`, `xs:NMTOKEN`, `xs:NMTOKENS`, `xs:normalizedString`, `xs:NOTATION`, `xs:QName`, `xs:string`, `xs:token`

Attributes

`value`
    An `xs:nonNegativeInteger`

Operation

For string values, the number in value specifies the number of Unicode characters allowed in the string. The number of Unicode characters is counted *after* whitespace processing is completed, per the rules of the datatype being constrained and the xs: whitespace facet.

For the xs:hexBinary and xs:base64Binary types, the value specifies the number of bytes encoded. When used in lists, the xs: length facet constrains the number of items in the list.

You cannot specify xs:length at the same time you specify xs: maxLength or xs:minLength.

xs:maxExclusive

Allows you to specify a maximum value below which all data in the type must remain

Applies to

xs:byte, xs:date, xs:dateTime, xs:decimal, xs:double, xs:duration, xs:float, xs:gDay, xs:gMonth, xs:gMonthDay, xs:gYear, xs: gYearMonth, xs:int, xs:integer, xs:long, xs:negativeInteger, xs: nonNegativeInteger, xs:nonPositiveInteger, xs:positiveInteger, xs:short, xs:time, xs:unsignedByte, xs:unsignedInt, xs: unsignedLong, xs:unsignedShort

Attributes

value
    An xs:nonNegativeInteger

Operation

For numeric values, the number in value specifies a number that no contents of that type may equal or exceed. Date and time values must be earlier than the specified xs:maxExclusive value.

You cannot specify xs:maxExclusive at the same time you specify xs:maxInclusive.

xs:maxInclusive

Allows you to specify a maximum value that all data in the type must be equal to or less than

Applies to

xs:byte, xs:date, xs:dateTime, xs:decimal, xs:double, xs:duration, xs:float, xs:gDay, xs:gMonth, xs:gMonthDay, xs:gYear, xs:gYearMonth, xs:int, xs:integer, xs:long, xs:negativeInteger, xs:nonNegativeInteger, xs:nonPositiveInteger, xs:positiveInteger, xs:short, xs:time, xs:unsignedByte, xs:unsignedInt, xs:unsignedLong, xs:unsignedShort

Attributes

value
    An xs:nonNegativeInteger

Operation

For numeric values, the number in value specifies a number that no contents of that type may exceed. Date and time values must be earlier than or equal to the specified xs:maxInclusive value.

You cannot specify xs:maxExclusive at the same time you specify xs:maxInclusive.

xs:maxLength

Allows you to specify the maximum length (in characters, bytes, or list items) of a given value

Applies to

xs:anyURI, xs:base64binary, xs:ENTITIES, xs:ENTITY, xs:hexBinary, xs:ID, xs:IDREF, xs:IDREFS, xs:language, xs:Name, xs:NCName, xs:NMTOKEN, xs:NMTOKENS, xs:normalizedString, xs:NOTATION, xs:QName, xs:string, xs:token

Attributes

value
    An xs:nonNegativeInteger

Operation

For string values, the number in value specifies the maximum number of Unicode characters allowed in the string. The number of Unicode characters is counted *after* whitespace processing is completed per the rules of the datatype being constrained and the xs:whitespace facet.

For the xs:hexBinary and xs:base64Binary types, the value specifies the maximum number of bytes encoded. When used in lists, the value constrains the number of items in the list.

You cannot specify xs:maxLength at the same time you specify xs:length or xs:minLength.

---

xs:minExclusive

Allows you to specify a minimum value above which all data in the type must remain

Applies to

xs:byte, xs:date, xs:dateTime, xs:decimal, xs:double, xs:duration, xs:float, xs:gDay, xs:gMonth, xs:gMonthDay, xs:gYear, xs:gYearMonth, xs:int, xs:integer, xs:long, xs:negativeInteger, xs:nonNegativeInteger, xs:nonPositiveInteger, xs:positiveInteger, xs:short, xs:time, xs:unsignedByte, xs:unsignedInt, xs:unsignedLong, xs:unsignedShort

Attributes

value
    An xs:nonNegativeInteger

Operation

For numeric values, the number in value specifies a number that no contents of that type may be equal to or less than. Date and time values must be later than the specified xs:minExclusive value.

You cannot specify xs:minExclusive at the same time you specify xs:minInclusive.

---

xs:minInclusive

Allows you to specify a maximum value that all data in the type must be equal to or less than

Applies to

xs:byte, xs:date, xs:dateTime, xs:decimal, xs:double, xs:duration, xs:float, xs:gDay, xs:gMonth, xs:gMonthDay, xs:gYear, xs:gYearMonth, xs:int, xs:integer, xs:long, xs:negativeInteger, xs:nonNegativeInteger, xs:nonPositiveInteger, xs:positiveInteger, xs:short, xs:time, xs:unsignedByte, xs:unsignedInt, xs:unsignedLong, xs:unsignedShort

Attributes

value
    An xs:nonNegativeInteger

Operation

For numeric values, the number in value specifies a number that no contents of that type may be below. Date and time values must be later than or equal to the specified xs:minInclusive value.

You cannot specify xs:minExclusive at the same time you specify xs:minInclusive.

xs:minLength

Allows you to specify the minimum length (in characters, bytes, or list items) of a given value

Applies to

xs:anyURI, xs:base64binary, xs:ENTITIES, xs:ENTITY, xs:hexBinary, xs:ID, xs:IDREF, xs:IDREFS, xs:language, xs:Name, xs:NCName, xs:NMTOKEN, xs:NMTOKENS, xs:normalizedString, xs:NOTATION, xs:QName, xs:string, xs:token

Attributes

value
    An xs:nonNegativeInteger

Operation

For string values, the number in value specifies the minimum number of Unicode characters allowed in the string. The number of Unicode characters is counted *after* whitespace processing is completed per the rules of the datatype being constrained and the xs:whitespace facet.

For the xs:hexBinary and xs:base64Binary types, the value specifies the minimum number of bytes encoded. When used in lists, the value constrains the minimum number of items in the list.

You cannot specify xs:minLength at the same time you specify xs:maxLength or xs:length.

xs:pattern

Allows you to specify value constraints using a regular expression

Applies to

All datatypes

Attributes

value

> An xs:string containing a regular expression defined using the rules set out in *http://www.w3.org/TR/xmlschema-2/#regexs*

Operation

During validation, the XML Schema processor compares the value of the element or attribute against the regular expression specified in the value attribute of the xs:pattern element. If the regular expression matches the content, the content is valid; otherwise, it's not. (If multiple xs:pattern facets are specified, the content is valid if it matches *any* of them.) The incredible flexibility of regular expressions makes it possible to create a wide variety of types that include mixed text and numbers, as well as types that must have particular patterns of punctuation.

XML Schema regular expressions operate in much the same way as regular expressions in Perl 5.6 and later, except that they implicitly anchor the expressions at the head and tail. To avoid this behavior, include the characters .* at the beginning or end of the expression. Tables 2–4 list the most commonly used aspects of XML Schema regular expressions as well as some Unicode-specific material that's much more frequently used in XML Schema processing than in other uses of regular expressions.

Table 2. Commonly used regular expression constructs

Pattern	Meaning
(String)	A value that matches String
String1 | String2	A value that matches String1 or String2
String?	Zero or one occurrence of String
String*	Zero or more occurrences of String
String+	One or more occurrences of String
String{num1, num2}	A sequence of String occurrences, with num1 to num2 repetitions
String{num1}	A sequence of exactly num1 occurrences of String
String{num1,}	A sequence of at least num1 occurrences of String
[char1char2...]	One of the characters listed in the square brackets
[^char1char2...]	One character not listed in the square brackets
[char1-char2]	One character in the Unicode range between char1 and char2
[char1-char2-[char3-char4]]	One character in the Unicode range between char1 and char2, but excluding the range between char3 and char4

TIP

You can use character and entity references in regular expressions. The XML parser will expand these references before the XML Schema processor works on them. Don't use references as a form of escaping, however. That only works for newlines, carriage returns, and tabs, and even here the results are not very readable. Instead, use the escape sequences listed in Table 3.

Table 3. Escape sequences and character classes for use in regular expressions

Sequence	Meaning
.	Any valid XML character except newlines and carriage returns
\n	The newline character (#xA)
\r	The return character (#xD)
\t	The tab character (#x9)
\\	\
|		
\.	.
\-	-
\^	^
\?	?
*	*
\+	+
\{	{
\}	}
\(	(
\)	)
\[	[
\]	]
\s	Spaces: space (#x20), tab (#x9), line feed (#xA), and carriage return (#xD)
\S	Anything that isn't a space as defined above
\d	Digits, including the Western 0–9 and digits in other Unicode alphabets
\D	Anything that isn't a digit as defined above
\w	A word character, which in Unicode means it isn't punctuation, separator, or other
\W	Anything that isn't a word character as defined above

Table 3. Escape sequences and character classes for use in regular expressions (continued)

Sequence	Meaning
\i	Any character allowed at the start of an XML name—generally letters and the underscore
\I	Any character not allowed at the start of an XML name
\c	Any character allowed in an XML name
\C	Any character not allowed in an XML name
\p{*UnicodeClass*}	Any character in the *UnicodeClass* (see Table 4)
\P{*UnicodeClass*}	Any character not in the *UnicodeClass* (see Table 4)
\p{Is*UnicodeBlock*}	Any character in the *UnicodeBlock* (see the list of Unicode character blocks, later in this section)
\P{Is*UnicodeBlock*}	Any character not in the *UnicodeBlock* (see the list of Unicode character blocks, later in this section)

Table 4. Unicode character classes for use in regular expressions

Class	Contents
C	All non-letters, non-symbols, non-separators, and non-numbers
Cc	Control characters
Cf	Format characters
Cn	Code points which are not assigned
Co	Code points in the Private Use Area
L	All letters
Ll	Lowercase letters
Lm	Modifiers
Lo	Other letters
Lt	Titlecase letters
Lu	Uppercase letters
M	All marks
Mc	Spacing combining marks
Me	Enclosing marks

Table 4. Unicode character classes for use in regular
expressions (continued)

Class	Contents
Mn	Non-spacing marks
N	All numbers
Nd	Decimal digits
Nl	Number letters
No	Other numbers
P	All punctuation characters
Pc	Connector punctuation
Pd	Dash punctuation
Pe	Closed punctuation
Pf	Final quotes
Pi	Initial quotes
Po	Other punctuation
Ps	Open punctuation
S	All symbols
Sc	Currency symbols
Sk	Modifier symbols
Sm	Math symbols
So	Other symbols
Z	All separators
Zl	Line separators
Zp	Paragraph separators
Zs	Spaces

To determine which characters fall into these categories, you'll need to refer to the Unicode specifications or the Unicode Character Database, available from *http://unicode.org/*. Also, you cannot match on the Cs class, which contains Unicode surrogates.

Following is a list of Unicode character blocks:

AlphabeticPresentationForms
Arabic
ArabicPresentationForms-A
ArabicPresentationForms-B
Armenian
Arrows
BasicLatin
Bengali
BlockElements
Bopomofo
BopomofoExtended
BoxDrawing
BraillePatterns
Cherokee
CJKCompatibility
CJKCompatibilityForms
CJKCompatibilityIdeographs
CJKRadicalsSupplement
CJKSymbolsandPunctuation
CJKUnifiedIdeographs
CJKUnifiedIdeographsExtensionA
CombiningDiacriticalMarks
CombiningHalfMarks
CombiningMarksforSymbols
ControlPictures
CurrencySymbols
Cyrillic
Devanagari
Dingbats
EnclosedAlphanumerics
EnclosedCJKLettersandMonths
Ethiopic
GeneralPunctuation
GeometricShapes
Georgian
Greek

HangulSyllables
Hebrew
Hiragana
IdeographicDescriptionCharacters
IPAExtensions
Kanbun
KangxiRadicals
Kannada
Katakana
Khmer
Lao
Latin-1Supplement
LatinExtended-A
LatinExtendedAdditional
LatinExtended-B
LetterlikeSymbols
Malayalam
MathematicalOperators
MiscellaneousSymbols
MiscellaneousTechnical
Mongolian
Myanmar
NumberForms
Ogham
OpticalCharacterRecognition
Oriya
PrivateUse
Runic
Sinhala
SmallFormVariants
SpacingModifierLetters
Specials
SuperscriptsandSubscripts
Syriac
Tamil
Telugu

GreekExtended	Thaana
Gujarati	Thai
Gurmukhi	Tibetan
HalfwidthandFullwidthForms	UnifiedCanadianAboriginalSyllabics
HangulCompatibilityJamo	YiRadicals
HangulJamo	YiSyllables

xs:totalDigits

Allows you to specify the number of significant digits used in a value

Applies to

xs:byte, xs:decimal, xs:int, xs:integer, xs:long, xs:negativeInteger,
xs:nonNegativeInteger, xs:nonPositiveInteger, xs:positiveInteger,
xs:short, xs:time, xs:unsignedByte, xs:unsignedInt, xs:unsignedLong,
xs:unsignedShort

Attributes

value
    An xs:nonNegativeInteger

Operation

The number in value specifies the number of significant digits
allowed in the number contained by the type. Despite the presence of other numeric types, xs:totalDigits is only available for
use with xs:decimal and types containing integer values.

xs:whiteSpace

Allows you to specify how whitespace processing should be performed on the contents of
a type

Applies to

xs:normalizedString, xs:string

Attributes

value
    One of preserve, replace, or collapse

Operation

This facet determines how the schema processor will report whitespace contained in string values. If the value attribute is set to preserve, all whitespace will be kept unchanged. If the value attribute is set to replace, all whitespace characters—including #x9 (tab), #xA (line feed), #xD (carriage return), and #x20 (space)—will be replaced with space characters. If the value attribute is set to collapse, every sequence of whitespace characters will be replaced with a single space.

Datatypes may also perform their own whitespace processing, but once whitespace is discarded through replace or collapse, which is the case for all types except xs:string and xs:normalizedString, it cannot be recovered.

XML Schema Attributes for Use in Instance Documents

While many developers create XML Schemas and use them to validate all documents which come through a given application, there are times when applications may prefer to work with information stored in the document instance, much as the DOCTYPE declaration of an XML document identifies the DTD against which that document should be validated and may include extra information extending that DTD. XML Schema supports both instance document information that points to external schemas for validation and two pieces that let document parts specify more precisely what their contents are.

All of these attributes are in the http://www.w3.org/2001/XMLSchema-instance namespace. There is no mechanism in XML Schema for constraining where these attributes may appear. In some sense, though they appear in a document instance that is validated with an XML Schema, these attributes are more document-specific supplements to the schema processing than they are parts of the document.

xsi:nil

The xsi:nil attribute is used to permit cases in which an element explicitly indicates that it doesn't have any content. If an empty element includes an xsi:nil="true" attribute, and if the declaration indicates that the element is nillable, the schema processor will accept the element as valid even if the schema requires that element to have content.

xsi:noNamespaceSchemaLocation

The xsi:noNamespaceSchemaLocation attribute gives the schema processor a hint, which the processor may ignore, about where to find a schema for the content of a document without a namespace. The value of the attribute is a URI (or list of URIs) wherein a schema for processing the document may be found.

xsi:schemaLocation

The xsi:schemaLocation attribute gives the schema processor a hint, which the processor may ignore, about where to find a schema for the content of a document that uses a particular namespace. The value of the attribute is a list containing an even number of URIs. The first URI of each pair is the namespace URI to which the schema applies, while the second URI of each pair identifies where to find a schema for processing the document.

xsi:type

The xsi:type attribute lets you define the type of an element locally (in the document) rather than in the schema. As XML Schema Part 1: Structures puts it, "An element information item in an instance may, however, explicitly assert its type using the attribute xsi:type."

The value of the xsi:type attribute must be a QName, identifying the type of the element. The type specified by xsi:type has to be a subtype of the type that was declared for the element originally. For the xsi:type declaration to work, a matching type must be defined in the schema the validator is using. Most typically, the xsi:type attribute is used to specify predefined types, but it isn't limited to that.

RELAX NG

RELAX NG is a simple yet elegant schema language for XML. It was developed at OASIS under the leadership of James Clark and Murata Makoto and grew out of earlier efforts on the schema languages TREX (by Clark) and RELAX (by Murata). After becoming an OASIS committee specification in late 2001, RELAX NG was later standardized under ISO's Document Schema Definition Languages (DSDL) effort as ISO/IEC 19757-2.

RELAX NG is easy to learn, easy to use, and is supported by a broad variety of free tools. It can be expressed in XML syntax or in a compact, non-XML syntax. Its use is certainly not as widespread as W3C XML Schema, but RELAX NG continues to be a favorite among XML experts.

The RELAX NG XML-syntax tutorial is at *http://relaxng.org/tutorial-20011203.html*; the compact-syntax tutorial is at *http://relaxng.org/compact-tutorial-20030326.html*; and the specification is at *http://relaxng.org/spec-20011203.html*. For more information, see *http://relaxng.org* and *http://dsdl.org*. Eric van der Vlist's *RELAX NG* (O'Reilly) is also an excellent resource (an online version is available at *http://books.xmlschemata.org/relaxng/*). The following material is intended for quick reference on usage and syntax. For a complete, detailed reference, I recommend Chapters 17 and 18 of van der Vlist's *RELAX NG*.

The following RELAX NG reference is organized by XML element name; an associated compact syntax is provided in an example for each. The element names in headings are prefixed with rng: to distinguish them from XML Schema elements with identical names; however, the prefix is not normally necessary in common usage, nor is it used in provided examples.

The datatypeLibrary and ns attributes are legal on all elements, though in some instances they have no effect. datatypeLibrary names the datatype library to be used in the schema, and ns specifies the default namespace for either the element or attribute, depending on context. It is common to specify the W3C XML Schema datatype namespace (*http://www.w3.org/2001/XMLSchema-datatypes*) as a datatype library. Compact syntax processors automatically bind this namespace to the prefix xsd:.

The RELAX NG namespace (*http://relaxng.org/ns/structure/1.0*) must be declared in schemas using the XML syntax; however, it need not be declared in the compact syntax, as compact syntax processors handle it internally. The namespace declaration is left out of most of the XML examples in order to reduce clutter.

When processed by a RELAX NG processor, elements and attributes from foreign namespaces are discarded. This means you can intermix elements or attributes from any namespace in RELAX NG schemas, such as XHTML, which makes it easy to add documentation to them.

Under the "Parents" heading, any element name in **`constant width bold italic`** may be a parent in the context of a name class; *all* elements named may be used in the context of a pattern. In this part of the book, numbers preceded by a section sign (§) under "See also" headings refer to sections in the RELAX NG XML-syntax tutorial (*http://relaxng.org/tutorial-20011203.html*).

rng:anyName

Specifies a name pattern that matches any name in any namespace

XML syntax example

```
<grammar xmlns="http://relaxng.org/ns/structure/1.0">

<start>
 <ref name="any"/>
</start>

<define name="any">
 <element>
  <anyName/>
  <zeroOrMore>
   <choice>
    <attribute>
     <anyName/>
    </attribute>
    <text/>
    <ref name="any"/>
   </choice>
  </zeroOrMore>
 </element>
</define>

</grammar>
```

Compact syntax example

```
start = any
any = element * { (attribute * { text } | text | any)* }
```

Parents

attribute, *choice*, *element*, *except*

Description

The anyName element, when used as the child of an attribute or element pattern, causes that pattern to match any element or attribute name from any namespace in an instance. You can also use anyName in conjunction with the except and nsName elements to exclude names in a given namespace.

See also

§11, except, nsName

---

rng:attribute

Matches an attribute

XML syntax example

```
<element name="date">
 <attribute name="year"/>
 <attribute name="month"/>
 <attribute name="day"/>
</element>
```

Compact syntax example

```
element date {
 attribute year { text },
 attribute month { text },
 attribute day { text }
}
```

Attributes

name

> An attribute name. If this name has a prefix, the namespace of the attribute is the namespace bound to that schema; if not, the attribute is in no namespace.

Parents

attribute, choice (( ) and |), define (name of pattern followed
by =), element, except (-), group (( ) and ,), interleave (&), list,
mixed, oneOrMore (+), optional (?), start (start followed by =),
zeroOrMore (*)

Description

The attribute pattern matches an attribute in an instance. If an
attribute element is empty, it is assumed to contain a text
pattern, so the following attribute patterns are equivalent:

```
<attribute name="greeting" />
```

```
<attribute name="greeting"><text/></attribute>
```

The name attribute is not required; you can specify a name with
the name child element, or a name class with an anyName, an nsName,
or a choice child element. In other words, instead of this:

```
<attribute name="date"/>
```

You could use this:

```
<attribute>
  <name>date</name>
</attribute>
```

However, you cannot use the name attribute and a name child
element at the same time; they are mutually exclusive. There is no
distinction between the name attribute and a name child element in
the compact syntax.

See also

§3, element, name

rng:choice

Matches one of a choice of patterns or name classes

XML syntax example

```
<choice>
 <element name="date"><text/></element>
 <element name="name"><text/></element>
 <element name="purpose"><text/></element>
</choice>
```

Compact syntax example

```
(element date { text }
 | element name { text }
 | element purpose { text })
```

Parents

attribute, *choice*, define, *element*, *except*, group, interleave, list, mixed, oneOrMore, optional, start, zeroOrMore

Description

The choice pattern matches one of a set of patterns, such as elements or attributes, or one of a set of name classes, such as names in a given namespace.

See also

§2, group, interleave

---

rng:data

Matches data of a given datatype

XML syntax example

```
<element name="num">
  <data type="decimal"
    datatypeLibrary="http://www.w3.org/2001/XMLSchema-
    datatypes">
   <param name="minInclusive">0.0</param>
   <param name="maxInclusive">1.0</param>
  </data>
</element>
```

Compact syntax example

```
element num {
  xsd:decimal { minInclusive = "0.0" maxInclusive = "1.0" }
}
```

Parents

attribute, choice (( ) and |), define (name of pattern followed by =), element, except (-), group (( ) and ,), interleave (&), list, mixed, oneOrMore (+), optional (?), start (start followed by =), zeroOrMore (*)

Attributes

type

> A datatype from the datatype library specified with the nearest datatypeLibrary attribute

Description

The data pattern matches any legal value of a specified datatype. An external datatype library, such as the XML Schema datatype library, defines the datatype. The datatype library is specified by the value of the datatypeLibrary attribute. Child or descendent elements inherit the value of datatypeLibrary; hence datatypeLibrary is often specified on the document element. Datatypes can be restricted using the param element. In the compact syntax, datatypes are specified by a name with a prefix. If no value is given for datatypeLibrary, RELAX NG defaults to a built-in datatype library with only two types: string and token. You can remove a value or a subtype from a datatype by using except.

See also

§5, except, list, param

rng:define

Defines a named pattern

XML syntax example

```
<grammar xmlns="http://relaxng.org/ns/structure/1.0">

<start>
 <ref name="greeting"/>
</start>

<define name="greeting">
 <choice>
  <element name="hello"><text/></element>
  <element name="hi"><text/></element>
  <element name="wazzup"><text/></element>
 </choice>
</define>

</grammar>
```

Compact syntax example

```
start = greeting
greeting = element hello { text }
  | element hi { text }
  | element wazzup { text }
```

Attributes

combine (|= for choice, &= for interleave)

> Valid values are choice or interleave. choice means multiple define elements are combined as a choice; interleave means multiple define elements are combined by interleaving.

name

> Specifies the name assigned to the pattern; must not have a prefix.

Parents

div, grammar, include

Description

The define element defines a named pattern that can be referenced by ref elsewhere in the schema or by parentRef to reference a named pattern in a parent schema. If define is in an include, it redefines any named pattern of the same name in the included schema unless the combine attribute is used (if you want to combine, you need to locate your new definitions *outside* of the include pattern). If multiple child patterns are present, they are treated as if wrapped by a group pattern. In the compact syntax, definitions can constitute the whole of a schema, as if a grammar pattern were present. Also in the compact syntax, choice and interleave combined definitions are expressed using |= and &= rather than simply =.

See also

§4, parentRef, ref

---

rng:div

Groups definitions for documentation purposes

XML syntax example

```
<grammar xmlns:doc="http://simonstl.com/ns/doc"
xmlns="http://relaxng.org/ns/structure/1.0">

<start>
 <ref name="greeting"/>
</start>

<div doc:note="This section says 'hello.'">
<define name="greeting" combine="choice">
 <element name="hello"><text/></element>
</define>
</div>

<div doc:note="This section says 'hi.'">
<define name="greeting" combine="choice">
 <element name="hi"><text/></element>
</define>
</div>

</grammar>
```

Compact syntax example

```
namespace doc = "http://simonstl.com/ns/doc"

start = greeting
[ doc:note = "This section says 'hello.'" ]
div {
  greeting |= element hello { text }
}
[ doc:note = "This section says 'hi.'" ]
div {
  greeting |= element hi { text }
}
```

Parents

div, grammar

Description

The div element allows you to divide a list of definitions into modules, primarily for documentation purposes. RELAX NG processors essentially disregard the div element. div elements may contain other div elements.

See also

§12

---

rng:element

Matches an element

XML syntax example

```
<element name="description">
 <data type="string"/>
</element>
```

Compact syntax example

```
element description { string }
```

Attributes

name

> An element name. If this name has a prefix, the namespace of the element is the namespace bound to that schema. Otherwise, the namespace is specified by the nearest enclosing ns attribute.

Parents

attribute, choice (( ) and |), define (name of pattern followed by =), element, except (-), group (( ) and ,), interleave (&), list, mixed, oneOrMore (+), optional (?), start (start followed by =), zeroOrMore (*)

Description

The element pattern matches an element in an instance. The name attribute is not required—you can specify a name with the name child element or specify a name class with an anyName, an nsName, or a choice child element. In other words, instead of this:

```
<element name="description"/>
```

You could use this:

```
<element>
 <name>description</name>
</element>
```

However, you cannot use the name attribute and a name child element at the same time; they are mutually exclusive. There is no distinction between the name attribute and a name child element in the compact syntax. If multiple child patterns are present, they are treated as if wrapped by a group pattern.

See also

§1, attribute, name

---

rng:empty

Specifies that the content of an element is empty

XML syntax example

```
<element name="photo">
 <attribute name="source"/>
 <empty/>
</element>
```

Compact syntax example

```
element photo { attribute source { text }, empty }
```

Parents

attribute, choice (( ) and |), define (name of pattern followed by =), element, except (-), group (( ) and ,), interleave (&), list, mixed, oneOrMore (+), optional (?), start (start followed by =), zeroOrMore (*)

Description

The empty pattern specifies empty content for an element. In RELAX NG, an element is considered empty if it contains whitespace only.

See also

§3, §10.1, element

rng:except

Excludes names or values

XML syntax example

```
<element name="digit"
  datatypeLibrary="http://www.w3.org/2001/XMLSchema-
  datatypes">
 <data type="nonPositiveInteger">
  <param name="minInclusive">-9</param>
  <except><value>0</value></except>
 </data>
</element>
```

Compact syntax example

```
element digit {
  xsd:nonPositiveInteger { minInclusive = "-9" } - ("0")
}
```

Parents

anyName, data, *nsName*

Description

The except element removes names from a name class or values from a datatype. When used with data, the data element can contain only other data, value, or choice elements. You can't use except to create an empty name class.

See also

§11, anyName, data, nsName, value

---

rng:externalRef

References an external schema

XML syntax example

```
<element name="date" xmlns="http://relaxng.org/ns/
  structure/1.0">
 <interleave>
  <element name="year">
   <list>
    <choice>
```

```
    <value>2002</value>
    <value>2003</value>
    <value>2004</value>
    <value>2005</value>
    <value>2006</value>
    <value>2007</value>
   </choice>
  </list>
 </element>
 <externalRef href="month.rng"/>
 <externalRef href="day.rng"/>
 </interleave>
 </element>
```

Compact syntax example

```
element date {
  element year {
    list { "2002" | "2003" | "2004" | "2005" | "2006" |
    "2007" }
  }
  & external "month.rnc"
  & external "day.rnc"
}
```

Attributes

href
    The location of the external schema

Parents

attribute, choice (( ) and |), define (name of pattern followed
by =), element, except (-), group (( ) and ,), interleave (&), list,
mixed, oneOrMore (+), optional (?), start (start followed by =),
zeroOrMore (*)

Description

The externalRef pattern references an external schema, in effect
replacing the instance of the externalRef element with the content
of the external schema. The external schema must contain a
pattern.

See also

§9.1, include, parentRef, ref

rng:grammar

Container for the definitions of named patterns

XML syntax example

```
<grammar xmlns="http://relaxng.org/ns/structure/1.0">

<start>
 <element name="cd">
  <attribute name="title"/>
  <optional>
   <attribute name="artist"/>
  </optional>
  <ref name="content"/>
 </element>
</start>

<define name="content">
 <element name="playlist">
  <oneOrMore>
   <element name="song"><text/></element>
  </oneOrMore>
 </element>
</define>

</grammar>
```

Compact syntax example

```
start = element cd {
 attribute title { text }, attribute artist { text }?,
 content
}
content = element playlist { element song { text }+ }
```

Parents

attribute, choice (( ) and |), define (name of pattern followed by =), element, except (-), group (( ) and ,), interleave (&), list, mixed, oneOrMore (+), optional (?), start (start followed by =), zeroOrMore (*)

Description

A grammar pattern acts as a container for define elements, which define named patterns, and for a start element, which specifies the pattern that must be matched in order for the grammar element to be matched. (A grammar pattern may also contain only a section of schema.) It is common to use a grammar pattern as the document element of a RELAX NG schema, and in the compact syntax, a grammar pattern is assumed if the schema consists of definitions using =.

See also

§4, §9, §13, define, start

---

rng:group

Matches whatever its child patterns match in sequence

XML syntax example

```
<element name="mylist">
 <zeroOrMore>
  <element name="item">
   <choice>
    <element name="name">
     <text/>
    </element>
    <group>
     <element name="givenname">
      <text/>
     </element>
     <element name="familyname">
      <text/>
     </element>
    </group>
   </choice>
   <element name="e-mail">
    <text/>
   </element>
   <optional>
    <element name="description">
     <text/>
    </element>
   </optional>
  </element>
 </zeroOrMore>
</element>
```

Compact syntax example

```
element mylist {
  element item {
    (element name { text }
     | (element givenname { text },
        element familyname { text })),
    element e-mail { text },
    element description { text }?
  }*
}
```

Parents

attribute, choice (( ) and |), define (name of pattern followed
by =), element, except (-), group (( ) and ,), interleave (&), list,
mixed, oneOrMore (+), optional (?), start (start followed by =),
zeroOrMore (*)

Description

The group pattern matches whatever its child patterns match in
the order specified (order is disregarded for attribute patterns).
Multiple patterns within define, oneOrMore, zeroOrMore, optional,
list, or mixed elements are treated as if they were wrapped by a
group pattern.

See also

§2, choice, interleave

rng:include

Includes another grammar into the current grammar

XML syntax example

include.rng

```
<grammar xmlns="http://relaxng.org/ns/structure/1.0">

<include href="type.rng"/>

<start combine="choice">
 <ref name="type" />
</start>
```

```
<define name="type">
 <element name="type">
  <list>
   <choice>
    <value>html</value>
    <value>xhtml</value>
    <value>xml</value>
   </choice>
  </list>
 </element>
</define>

</grammar>
```

type.rng

```
<grammar xmlns="http://relaxng.org/ns/structure/1.0">

<start combine="choice">
 <element name="type">
  <list>
   <choice>
    <value>text</value>
    <value>other</value>
   </choice>
  </list>
 </element>
</start>

</grammar>
```

Compact syntax example

include.rnc

```
include "type.rnc"
start |= type
type = element type { list { "html" | "xhtml" | "xml" } }
```

type.rnc

```
start |= element type { list { "text" | "other" } }
```

Attributes

href
> The location of the grammar to include

Parents

div, grammar

Description

The include element includes another grammar in the current one. The included grammar must have a grammar element as the document element. Its rules are effectively merged with the including grammar. An include element may contain define elements that override or are combined with definitions of the same name in the including grammar.

See also

§9.3, grammar, start

---

rng:interleave

Matches patterns mixed in any order

XML syntax example

```
<grammar xmlns="http://relaxng.org/ns/structure/1.0">

<start>
 <element name="name">
  <ref name="name"/>
 </element>
</start>

<define name="name">
 <interleave>
  <element name="given">
   <text/>
  </element>
  <optional>
   <element name="middle">
    <text/>
   </element>
  </optional>
  <element name="family">
```

```
    <text/>
   </element>
  </interleave>
</define>

</grammar>
```

Compact syntax example

```
start = element name { name }
name = element given { text }
  & element middle { text }?
  & element family { text }
```

Parents

attribute, choice (( ) and |), define (name of pattern followed
by =), element, except (-), group (( ) and ,), interleave (&), list,
mixed, oneOrMore (+), optional (?), start (start followed by =),
zeroOrMore (*)

Description

The interleave pattern interleaves its children. Its most common
use is for matching unordered content. interleave containing a
text node matches mixed content. An interleave element may
contain only one child element that directly or indirectly contains
a text element (this avoids combinatorial explosion). Also, it is
not possible to interleave data, value, or list patterns with child
element or text patterns. RELAX NG does not require deterministic content models as do XML Schema and DTDs.

See also

§8, group, mixed, oneOrMore, optional, zeroOrMore

---

rng:list

Breaks an element's character content or an attribute value into whitespace-separated strings

XML syntax example

```
<element name="type" datatypeLibrary="http://www.w3.org/
2001/XMLSchema-datatypes">
<attribute name="values">
 <list>
  <data type="int"/>
```

```
      <data type="int"/>
      <data type="int"/>
    </list>
  </attribute>
  <empty/>
</element>
```

Compact syntax example

```
element type {
  attribute values { list { xsd:int, xsd:int, xsd:int } },
  empty
}
```

Parents

attribute, choice (( ) and |), define (name of pattern followed by =), element, except (-), group (( ) and ,), interleave (&), list, mixed, oneOrMore (+), optional (?), start (start followed by =), zeroOrMore (*)

Description

The list pattern matches a whitespace-separated list of values in an instance. list actually splits text nodes into tokens separated by whitespace, which allows each token to be matched individually by a RELAX NG pattern. If multiple child patterns are present, they are treated as if they were wrapped by a group pattern. To match possible multiple tokens, a list pattern should contain an explicit or implicit group pattern, a zeroOrMore pattern, or a oneOrMore pattern.

See also

§7, param, text, value

---

rng:mixed

Matches a pattern with mixed element and text content

XML syntax example

```
<element name="para">
  <mixed>
   <zeroOrMore>
    <choice>
     <element name="italic"><text/></element>
```

```
    <element name="bold"><text/></element>
   </choice>
  </zeroOrMore>
 </mixed>
</element>
```

Compact syntax example

```
element para {
  mixed { (element italic { text } | element bold {
          text })*}
}
```

Parents

attribute, choice (( ) and |), define (name of pattern followed
by =), element, except (-), group (( ) and ,), interleave (&), list,
mixed, oneOrMore (+), optional (?), start (start followed by =),
zeroOrMore (*)

Description

The mixed pattern matches a pattern of mixed text and elements in
an instance. It is a shortcut for using the interleave element with
a text element. The text element is assumed in mixed. If multiple
child patterns are present, they are treated as if they were wrapped
by a group pattern.

See also

§8, element, interleave, text

rng:name

Specifies a name pattern which matches a name

XML syntax example

```
<element>
 <name>desc</name>
 <optional><attribute name="type"/></optional>
 <text/>
</element>
```

Compact syntax example

```
element desc { attribute type { text }?, text }
```

Parents

attribute, *choice*, *element*, *except*

Description

The name element specifies a name class that contains a specific name in a specific namespace. When used as the direct child of an element or attribute pattern, it is an alternative for the name attribute on element or attribute. However, you can't use both at the same time—they are mutually exclusive.

See also

§11, attribute, element

---

rng:notAllowed

Fails when matched

XML syntax example

```
<element name="abstract">
    <notAllowed/>
</element>
```

Compact syntax example

```
element abstract { notAllowed }
```

Parents

attribute, choice (( ) and |), define (name of pattern followed by =), element, except (-), group (( ) and ,), interleave (&), list, mixed, oneOrMore (+), optional (?), start (start followed by =), zeroOrMore (*)

Description

The notAllowed pattern fails when matched. In grammars that will be incorporated into larger grammars, notAllowed is useful for specifying an abstract pattern that may be overridden.

See also

§13

---

rng:nsName

Specifies a name pattern that matches any name in a specified namespace

XML syntax example

```
<grammar xmlns="http://relaxng.org/ns/structure/1.0">

<start>
 <ref name="any"/>
</start>

<define name="any">
 <element>
  <nsName ns="http://simonstl.com/ns/address"/>
  <zeroOrMore>
   <choice>
    <attribute>
     <nsName ns="http://simonstl.com/ns/address"/>
    </attribute>
    <text/>
    <ref name="any"/>
   </choice>
  </zeroOrMore>
 </element>
</define>

</grammar>
```

Compact syntax example

```
namespace ad = "http://simonstl.com/ns/address"

start = any
any = element ad:* { (attribute ad:* { text } | text |
any)* }
```

Parents

attribute, *choice*, *element*, *except*

Description

The nsName element specifies a name pattern that matches any
name in a given namespace.

See also

§11, anyName, except, name

rng:oneOrMore

Matches one or more occurrences of whatever its children match

XML syntax example

```
<element name="dates" datatypeLibrary="http://www.w3.org/
 2001/XMLSchema-datatype">
 <oneOrMore>
  <element name="date">
   <data type="dateTime" />
  </element>
 </oneOrMore>
</element>
```

Compact syntax example

```
element dates { element date { xsd:dateTime }+ }
```

Parents

attribute, choice (( ) and |), define (name of pattern followed by =), element, except (-), group (( ) and ,), interleave (&), list, mixed, oneOrMore (+), optional (?), start (start followed by =), zeroOrMore (*)

Description

The oneOrMore pattern matches an instance with one or more children defined in oneOrMore. In the compact syntax, oneOrMore is represented by a plus sign, as in DTDs. oneOrMore cannot hold attribute element definitions. If multiple child patterns are present, they are treated as if they were wrapped by a group pattern.

See also

§1, optional, zeroOrMore

rng:optional

Matches zero or one occurrences of whatever its children match

XML syntax example

```
<element name="date"
 datatypeLibrary="http://www.w3.org/2001/XMLSchema-
 datatypes">
```

```
<optional>
 <element name="mydate">
  <data type="dateTime" />
 </element>
</optional>
</element>
```

Compact syntax example

```
element date { element mydate { xsd:dateTime }? }
```

Parents

attribute, choice (( ) and |), define (name of pattern followed by =), element, except (-), group (( ) and ,), interleave (&), list, mixed, oneOrMore (+), optional (?), start (start followed by =), zeroOrMore (*)

Description

The optional pattern matches a pattern of zero or one of whatever its children match. In the compact syntax, optional is represented by a question mark, as in DTDs. If multiple child patterns are present, they are treated as if they were wrapped by a group pattern.

See also

§1, oneOrMore, zeroOrMore

rng:param

Specifies a parameter for a datatype

XML syntax example

```
<element name="digit"
 datatypeLibrary="http://www.w3.org/2001/XMLSchema-
 datatypes">
 <data type="int">
  <param name="minInclusive">0</param>
  <param name="maxInclusive">9</param>
 </data>
</element>
```

Compact syntax example

```
element digit { xsd:int { minInclusive = "0" maxInclusive
= "9" } }
```

Attributes

name
> The name of the parameter (facet)

Parents

data

Description

The param element specifies a parameter that is associated with a datatype specified by a parent data element. These parameters are called *facets* in the context of XML Schema datatypes (Table 5). The XML Schema datatype library is the most common datatype library associated with a RELAX NG schema, though others are possible.

Table 5. XML Schema datatype facets

Facet	Description
length	Length in units
minLength	Minimum length in units
maxLength	Maximum length in units
pattern	A regular expression
minInclusive	Minimum inclusive value
maxInclusive	Maximum inclusive value
minExclusive	Minimum exclusive value
maxExclusive	Maximum exclusive value
totalDigits	Total number of digits
fractionDigits	Number of digits to the right of the decimal point

---

TIP

The enumeration and whitespace facets of XML Schema datatypes are not supported by RELAX NG.

See also

§5, data, list, value

---

rng:parentRef

References a named pattern in a parent grammar

XML syntax example

```
<grammar xmlns="http://relaxng.org/ns/structure/1.0">

<start>
 <choice>
  <ref name="type" />
  <ref name="alt" />
 </choice>
</start>

<define name="type">
 <element name="type">
  <list>
   <choice>
    <value>html</value>
    <value>xhtml</value>
    <value>xml</value>
   </choice>
  </list>
 </element>
</define>

<define name="alt">
 <grammar>
  <start>
  <choice>
   <element name="method">
```

```
    <list>
     <choice>
      <value>text</value>
      <value>other</value>
     </choice>
    </list>
   </element>
   <parentRef name="type"/>
  </choice>
  </start>
 </grammar>
</define>

</grammar>
```

Compact syntax example

```
start = type | alt
type = element type { list { "html" | "xhtml" | "xml" } }
alt = grammar { start =
 element method { list { "text" | "other" } } | parent
 type }
```

Parents

attribute, choice (( ) and |), define (name of pattern followed by =), element, except (-), group (( ) and ,), interleave (&), list, mixed, oneOrMore (+), optional (?), start (start followed by =), zeroOrMore (*)

Description

The parentRef pattern references a named pattern in a parent grammar—that is, a grammar that directly or indirectly contains the current grammar. parentRef extends the scope of the current grammar to definitions in the parent grammar.

See also

§13, externalRef, ref

rng:ref

Refers to a named pattern

XML syntax example

```
<grammar xmlns="http://relaxng.org/ns/structure/1.0">

<start>
 <ref name="torque"/>
</start>

<define name="torque">
 <element name="torque">
  <attribute name="value"/>
  <empty/>
 </element>
</define>

</grammar>
```

Compact syntax example

```
start = torque
torque = element torque { attribute value { text }, empty }
```

Parents

attribute, choice (( ) and |), define (name of pattern followed
by =), element, except (-), group (( ) and ,), interleave (&), list,
mixed, oneOrMore (+), optional (?), start (start followed by =),
zeroOrMore (*)

Description

The ref pattern refers to a named pattern in a define element. In
the compact syntax, a reference is made to a named pattern by
using the name of the pattern by itself. References may be recur-
sive (a ref within a named pattern may refer to itself) provided the
reference is directly or indirectly within an element pattern that is
contained in the definition.

See also

§4, define, externalRef, parentRef

rng:start

Specifies a pattern within a grammar that must be matched in order to match the whole `grammar` element

XML syntax example

```
<grammar xmlns="http://relaxng.org/ns/structure/1.0">

<start>
 <element name="date">
  <ref name="date"/>
 </element>
</start>

<define name="date">
 <interleave>
  <element name="month">
   <text/>
  </element>
  <element name="day">
   <text/>
  </element>
  <element name="year">
   <text/>
  </element>
 </interleave>
</define>

</grammar>
```

Compact syntax example

```
start = element date { date }
date = element month { text }
 & element day { text }
 & element year { text }
```

Attributes

combine (|= for choice, &= for interleave)

Used when grammars are included with include. Valid values are choice or interleave. choice means multiple start elements are selected as one of a choice; interleave means multiple start elements are interleaved.

Parents

div, grammar, include

Description

The start element specifies the pattern that must be matched in order for the grammar pattern that contains it to match. If the grammar pattern is the document element of the RELAX NG schema, then the start element specifies the document element of the instance being validated.

See also

§4, §9, grammar, include

---

rng:text

Matches textual content in elements or attributes

XML syntax example

```
<element name="description">
 <attribute name="type"><text/></attribute>
 <text/>
</element>
```

Compact syntax example

```
element description { attribute type { text }, text }
```

Parents

attribute, choice (( ) and |), define (name of pattern followed by =), element, except (-), group (( ) and ,), interleave (&), list, mixed, oneOrMore (+), optional (?), start (start followed by =), zeroOrMore (*)

Description

The text pattern matches textual content in elements or attributes. It can match any amount of text (i.e., any number of text nodes), including none at all; hence text, text?, text*, and text+ all mean the same thing.

See also

§1, data, param, value

rng:value

Matches a specific value, including a value from a specified datatype

XML syntax example

```
<element name="answer">
 <choice>
  <value>yes</value>
  <value>no</value>
  <value>true</value>
  <value>false</value>
 </choice>
</element>

<element name="value" datatypeLibrary="http://www.w3.org/
 2001/XMLSchema-datatypes">
 <choice>
  <value type="string">one</value>
  <value type="integer">1</value>
  <value type="decimal">1.0</value>
 </choice>
</element>
```

Compact syntax example

```
element answer { "yes" | "no" | "true" | "false" }

element value { xsd:string "one" | xsd:integer "1" | xsd:
decimal "1.0" }
```

Attributes

type

A datatype from the datatype library that is specified with the nearest datatypeLibrary attribute

Parents

attribute, choice (( ) and |), define (name of pattern followed by =), element, except (-), group (( ) and ,), interleave (&), list, mixed, oneOrMore (+), optional (?), start (start followed by =), zeroOrMore (*)

Description

The value pattern matches a specific value from an enumeration or, when using the type attribute, a value from a specific datatype. The value of the type attribute may match any legal value of a specified datatype library such as the XML Schema datatype library. The datatype library is specified by the value of the datatypeLibrary attribute. Child or descendant elements inherit the value of datatypeLibrary; hence datatypeLibrary is often specified on the document element. Datatypes can be restricted using the param element. In the compact syntax, the datatype is specified by a name with a prefix. If no value is given for datatypeLibrary, RELAX NG defaults to a built-in datatype library that has only two types: string and token.

See also

§6, data, list, param, text

rng:zeroOrMore

Matches zero or more occurrences of whatever its children match

XML syntax example

```
<element name="name">
 <element name="givenname"><text/></element>
 <zeroOrMore>
  <element name="middlename"><text/></element>
 </zeroOrMore>
 <element name="familyname"><text/></element>
</element>
```

Compact syntax example

```
element name {
  element givenname { text },
  element middlename { text }*,
  element familyname { text }
}
```

Parents

`attribute`, `choice` (`( )` and `|`), `define` (name of pattern followed by `=`), `element`, `except` (`-`), `group` (`( )` and `,`), `interleave` (`&`), `list`, `mixed`, `oneOrMore` (`+`), `optional` (`?`), `start` (start followed by `=`), `zeroOrMore` (`*`)

Description

The `zeroOrMore` pattern matches zero or more occurrences of its children in a schema. In the compact syntax, `zeroOrMore` is represented by `*`, as in DTDs. If multiple child patterns are present, they are treated as if they were wrapped by a `group` pattern.

See also

§1, `oneOrMore`, `optional`

Schematron

Schematron, which was developed by Rick Jelliffe, is a simple yet powerful schema language for XML and has recently become a an ISO standard candidate (ISO/IEC 19747-3; see *http://www.dsdl.org*). Schematron uses rule-based validation rather than the grammar-based validation used by XML Schema and RELAX NG, among others. It uses expressions written in XPath to precisely examine nodes in an instance, thus becoming, as Jelliffe puts it, the "feather duster" that can reach into corners where grammar-based languages cannot. Schematron is good at testing for co-occurrence constraints— that is, constraints based on the existence of a value or structure that in turn is based on the existence of another value or structure.

The most common version of Schematron is 1.5. You can obtain a reference implementation (an XSLT stylesheet) for Version 1.5 from *http://xml.ascc.net/schematron/1.5/*. A variety of Schematron validators are available from Topologi (*http://www.topologi.com/*). You can also get information on the new ISO Schematron and its implementations from *http://www.schematron.com/*.

An example of a Schematron 1.5 schema is shown in Example 13.

Example 13. horse.sch

```
1  <?xml version="1.0" encoding="US-ASCII"?>
2  <sch:schema xmlns:sch="http://www.ascc.net/xml/ schematron">
3    <sch:title>Horse schema</sch:title>
4    <sch:pattern>
5      <sch:rule context="horse">
6        <sch:assert test="@legs = '4'">Our horses should have
           4 legs.</sch:assert>
7        <sch:assert test="snip">Our horses should have a snip.
           </sch:report>
8        <sch:report test="blaze">This horse has a blaze.
           </sch:report>
9        <sch:report test="star">This horse has a star.
           </sch:report>
10     </sch:rule>
11   </sch:pattern>
12 </sch:schema>
```

Line 1 is simply an XML declaration. Line 2 is the root element of the schema that contains a namespace declaration. The namespace URI for Schematron 1.5 is *http://www.ascc. net/xml/schematron*; alternatively, the namespace is *http:// purl.oclc.org/dsdl/schematron* for the new ISO Schematron. The conventional prefix is sch:. Line 3 titles the schema with human-readable text in an optional title element. This is followed on line 4 by a pattern element.

A schema element must be followed by one or more pattern elements. The pattern element, which lays out a set of rules for validation, is followed by a rule element (line 5). rule elements list assertions about the given context. The context of the horse element (from the instance being validated) is given in the context attribute, which is required. Following this are four assertions: the two assert elements (lines 6 and 7) state constraints that are expected or required, and the two report elements (lines 8 and 9), using a reversed logic of that of the assert elements, identify exceptional data. A rule element usually contains assert and report elements. (It *must* be followed by one or more assert elements, one or more extends elements, or one or more report elements.) Each assert or report element specifies an assertion about the context in the required test attribute. (An extends element identifies abstract rules via an ID.) Here you have it—the basics of Schematron.

The remainder of this section provides a brief reference for ISO Schematron. Typically, to use Version 1.5 schemas as ISO schemas, you need only make a namespace change from *http://www.ascc.net/xml/schematron* to *http://purl.oclc.org/dsdl/schematron*.

The following elements allow common attributes: assert, diagnostic, pattern, phase, report, rule, schema, title. Common optional attributes include the following: icon = *URI*; see = *URI*; fpi = *string*; xml:lang = *text*; xml:space = ("preserve" | "default"). The following elements *cannot* contain foreign elements and attributes (that is, elements and attributes that are not in the Schematron namespace): emph, let, and param. extends, name, and ns permit foreign attributes but not foreign elements.

In this reference, the following items appear in parentheses: "required" means the element or attribute must appear where specified, + means the element may occur one or more times, ? means the element or attribute may occur once or not at all (i.e., it's optional), and * means the element may occur zero or more times.

Core Elements

These elements are listed in hierarchical order.

sch:schema

Top-level container element for a schema

Parents

Attributes

common; schemaVersion = *string* (?, non-empty); defaultPhase = *IDREF* (?); version = *string* (?, non-empty); language = *string* (?, non-empty)

Children

include (*), title (?), ns (*), p (*), let (*), phase (*), pattern (+), diagnostics (?)

---

sch:pattern

A set of rules or constraints for the schema

Parents

schema

Attributes

common; id = *ID* (?); abstract = ("true" (if true, required of course) | "false" (?)); is-a = *IDREF* (to match the *ID* of an abstract pattern)

Children

include (*), title (?), p (*), param (*), let (*), rule (*)

---

sch:rule

Lists assertions in a given context. An element node in the document matches only once per pattern in the first rule whose context attribute matches that node.

Parents

pattern

Attributes

common; id = *ID* (?); abstract = ("true" (if true, required of course) | "false" (?)); context = *path* (required if abstract = "false" or not present)

Children

assert (+) | extends (+) | report (+), include (*), let (*)

---

sch:assert

Lists an assertion about a context node

Parents

rule

Attributes

common; test = *expression* (required); flag = *NCName* (?); id = *ID* (?); diagnostics = *IDREFS* (?); role = *NCName* (?); subject = *string* (?)

Children

text, dir (*), emph (*), name (*), span (*)

Other Elements

---

sch:active

Refers to an active pattern in the current phase

Parents

phase

Attributes

pattern = *IDREF* (required)

Children

text (*), dir (*), emph (*), span (*)

---

sch:diagnostic

Details a failed assertion

Parents

diagnostics

Attributes

common; id = *ID* (required)

Children

text (*), dir (*), emph (*), span (*), value-of (*)

sch:diagnostics

Acts as a container for diagnostics

Parents

schema

Attributes

Children

include (*), diagnostic (*)

sch:dir

Direction (right or left) of natural text

Parents

active, assert, diagnostic, p, report, title

Attributes

value = "ltr" | "rtl" (?)

Children

text

sch:emph

Marks text to be rendered with emphasis

Parents

active, assert, diagnostic, p, report

Attributes

Children

text

sch:extends

Identifies abstract rules

Parents

rule

Attributes

rule = *IDREF* (required)

Children

empty

sch:include

References an external XML document with a schema fragment

Parents

diagnostics, pattern, phase, rule, schema

Attributes

src = *URI*

Children

empty

sch:let

Declares a named variable

Parents

schema, pattern, phase, rule

Attributes

name = *NCName* (required); value = *string* (required)

Children

empty

sch:name
Finds names of nodes

Parents
assert, report

Attributes
path = *string* (?)

Children
empty

---

sch:ns
Specifies a namespace URI and prefix. (Note that the @xmlns:* mechanism used to declare namespaces for elements and attributes is *not* used.)

Parents
schema

Attributes
prefix = *NCName* (required); uri = *namespace URI* (required)

Children
empty

---

sch:p
Indicates documentation text

Parents
pattern, phase, schema

Attributes
class = (?)

Children
dir (*), emph (*), span (*)

---

sch:param

Works as a simple macro structure in abstract patterns

Parents

patternfsabstract="true"

Attributes

name = *NCName* (required); value = *string* (required, non-empty)

Children

empty

---

sch:phase

Groups patterns together to allow validation of certain constraints (but denies validation to some others)

Parents

active

Attributes

common; id = *ID* (required)

Children

active (*), include (*), let (*), p (*)

---

sch:report

Similar to assert; makes negative assertion about context nodes

Parents

rule

Attributes

common; test = *expression* (required); flag = *NCName* (?); id = *ID* (?); diagnostics = *IDREFS* (?); role = *NCName* (?); subject = *string* (?)

Children

text, dir (*), emph (*), name (*), span (*)

---

sch:span

Marks text for rendering

Parents

active, assert, diagnostic, p, report

Attributes

class = *string* (?)

Children

text

sch:title

Summarizes the purpose or role of a schema or pattern

Parents

pattern, rule, schema

Attributes

common

Children

text, dir (*)

sch:value-of

Returns values from an XML document

Parents

assert, diagnostic, report

Attributes

select = *string* (required)

Children

empty

XML Specifications

The following list of XML-related specifications is by no means comprehensive but is provided as a quick reference to the URIs for prominent specs.

- XML 1.0 (Third Edition): *http://www.w3.org/TR/REC-xml*
- XML 1.1: *http://www.w3.org/TR/xml11*
- Namespaces in XML 1.0: *http://www.w3.org/TR/REC-xml-names*
- Namespaces in XML 1.1: *http://www.w3.org/TR/xml-names11*
- Resource Directory Description Language (RDDL): *http://www.rddl.org*
- Associating Stylesheets with XML 1.0: *http://www.w3.org/TR/xml-stylesheet*
- XML Information Set (Second Edition): *http://www.w3.org/TR/xml-infoset*
- XSLT 1.0: *http://www.w3.org/TR/xslt*
- XSLT 2.0: *http://www.w3.org/TR/xslt20*
- XPath 1.0: *http://www.w3.org/TR/xpath*
- XPath 2.0: *http://www.w3.org/TR/xpath20*
- XSL 1.0: *http://www.w3.org/TR/xsl*
- XSL 1.1: *http://www.w3.org/TR/xsl11*
- XQuery 1.0: *http://www.w3.org/TR/xquery*
- XQuery 1.0 and XPath 2.0 Data Model: *http://www.w3.org/TR/xpath-datamodel*
- XQuery 1.0 and XPath 2.0 Functions and Operators: *http://www.w3.org/TR/xpath-functions*
- XHTML 1.0 (Second Edition): *http://www.w3.org/TR/xhtml1*
- XHTML Basic: *http://www.w3.org/TR/xhtml-basic*
- XHTML Modularization: *http://www.w3.org/TR/xhtml-modularization*
- XHTML 1.1 (module-based): *http://www.w3.org/TR/xhtml11*

- XHTML 2.0: *http://www.w3.org/TR/xhtml2*
- Canonical XML 1.0: *http://www.w3.org/TR/xml-c14n*
- XML Schema 1.0 Primer (Second Edition): *http://www.w3.org/TR/xmlschema-0*
- XML Schema 1.0 Structures (Second Edition): *http://www.w3.org/TR/xmlschema-1*
- XML Schema 1.1 Structures: *http://www.w3.org/TR/xmlschema11-1*
- XML Schema 1.0 Datatypes (Second Edition): *http://www.w3.org/TR/xmlschema-2*
- XML Schema 1.1 Datatypes: *http://www.w3.org/TR/xmlschema11-2*
- RELAX NG tutorial: *http://relaxng.org/tutorial-20011203.html*
- RELAX NG compact syntax tutorial: *http://relaxng.org/compact-tutorial-20030326.html*
- RELAX NG specification: *http://relaxng.org/spec-20011203.html*
- RELAX NG compact syntax specification: *http://relaxng.org/compact-20021121.html*
- xml:id 1.0: *http://www.w3.org/TR/xml-id*
- XML Base 1.0: *http://www.w3.org/TR/xmlbase*
- XLink 1.0: *http://www.w3.org/TR/xlink*
- XLink 1.1: *http://www.w3.org/TR/xlink11*
- XInclude 1.0: *http://www.w3.org/TR/xinclude*
- Ruby Annotation: *http://www.w3.org/TR/ruby*
- Scalable Vector Graphics (SVG) 1.1: *http://www.w3.org/TR/SVG11*
- Scalable Vector Graphics (SVG) 1.2: *http://www.w3.org/TR/SVG12*
- Scalable Vector Graphics (SVG) Tiny 1.2: *http://www.w3.org/TR/SVGMobile12*

- XPointer Framework: *http://www.w3.org/TR/xptr-framework*
- XPointer element( ) Scheme: *http://www.w3.org/TR/xptr-element*
- XPointer xmlns( ) Scheme: *http://www.w3.org/TR/xptr-xmlns*
- XForms 1.0: *http://www.w3.org/TR/xforms*
- XForms 1.1: *http://www.w3.org/TR/xforms11*
- SAX (Simple API for XML) 2.0.1: *http://www.saxproject.org*
- XML Object Model (XOM) 1.0: *http://www.cafeconleche.org/XOM*
- XML Pull Parsing: *http://www.xmlpull.org*
- JSR 173: Streaming API for XML: *http://jcp.org/en/jsr/detail?id=173*
- DocBook: *http://www.docbook.org*
- Universal Business Language (UBL) 1.0: *http://docs.oasis-open.org/ubl/cd-UBL-1.0/*
- Universal Description, Discovery, and Integration (UDDI) 3.0.2: *http://uddi.org/pubs/uddi_v3.htm*
- RSS (Rich Site Summary) 0.91: *http://backend.userland.com/rss091*
- RSS (RDF Site Summary) 1.0: *http://web.resource.org/rss/1.0/spec*
- RSS (Really Simple Syndication) 2.0: *http://blogs.law.harvard.edu/tech/rss*
- Atom (an RFC): *http://www.ietf.org/internet-drafts/draft-ietf-atompub-format-08.txt*

Index

A

active element, Schematron, 154
all element, XML Schema, 64
ancestor element, 11
annotation element, XML
    Schema, 65
annotations, schemas, 63
anonymous type definitions,
    schemas, 54
any element, XML Schema, 65
anyAttribute element, XML
    Schema, 66
anyName element, RELAX
    NG, 119
anySimpleType element, XML
    Schema, 85
anyURL element, XML
    Schema, 85
appInfo element, XML
    Schema, 67
assert element, Schematron, 154
attribute element, RELAX
    NG, 120
attribute element, XML
    Schema, 67
attributeGroup element, XML
    Schema, 69

attribute-list declarations, 36
attributes, 13
    elements and, 14
    global, 51
    pseudo-attributes, 23
    xml:id, 28
    xml:lang, 27
    xml:space, 26
    xsi:nil, 117
    xsi:noNamespaceSchema-
        Location, 117
    xsi:schemaLocation, 117
    xsi:type, 117

B

base64binary element, XML
    Schema, 86
boolean element, XML
    Schema, 86
byte element, XML Schema, 87

C

case sensitivity, elements, 8
CDATA sections, 24
character references, 16
characters, 15

We'd like to hear your suggestions for improving our indexes. Send email to
index@oreilly.com.

child element, 11
choice element, RELAX
         NG, 121
choice element, XML
         Schema, 69
choice operator (|), DTDs, 36, 45
colons in elements, 8
comments, 4, 19
    DTDs, 44
    parsed character data, 19
complexContentelement, XML
         Schema, 70
complexType element, XML
         Schema, 70
compositors, 56
conditional sections, DTDs, 45
constraining facets, 102–116
content models, 35

D

data element, RELAX NG, 122
date element, XML Schema, 87
dateTime element, XML
         Schema, 87
decimal element, XML
         Schema, 88
declarations, 20
    attribute-list declarations, 36
    DOCTYPE, 24
    element types, 35
    encoding declarations, 21
    standalone document
         declarations, 22
    text, DTDs, 35
default values, schemas, 61
define element, RELAX NG, 123
descendant element, 11
diagnostic element,
         Schematron, 154
diagnostics element,
         Schematron, 155
dir element, Schematron, 155

div element, RELAX NG, 125
DOCTYPE (document type
         declarations), 4, 24
documennts
    DOCTYPEs, 25
document (root) element, 10
documentation element, XML
         Schema, 72
documents
    DOCTYPEs, 4
    DTDs, 4, 33
    example of simple, 4
    well-formed, 3
double element, XML
         Schema, 88
DTDs (document type
         definition), 4, 32–47
    attribute-list declarations, 36
    comments, 44
    conditional sections, 45
    content models, 35
    element type declarations, 35
    external subsets, 33
      with internal, 39
    internal subsets, 37
      with external, 39
    namespaces, emulation, 37
    notations, 45
    parameter entities, 33, 43
    parsed entities, 41
    system identifiers, 34
    text declaration, 35
    unparsed entities, 45
duration element, XML
         Schema, 89

E

element element, RELAX
         NG, 126
element element, XML
         Schema, 72
element type declarations, 35

elements, 6–13
  ancestor element, 11
  attributes and, 14
  case sensitivity, 8
  child element, 11
  colons, 8
  compositors, 56
  descendant element, 11
  empty-element tags, 9
  end-tags, 8
  global, 51
  leaf element, 11
  mixed content, 12
  nesting, 9
  parent element, 11
  RELAX NG element, 137
  root element, 10
  sibling elements, 11
  start-tags, 8
emph element, Schematron, 155
empty content, XML
    Schema, 61
empty element, RELAX
    NG, 127
empty-element tags, 9
encoding declarations, 21
end-tags, 8
ENTITIES element, XML
    Schema, 90
ENTITY element, XML
    Schema, 90
entity references, 16
enumeration element, XML
    Schema, 103
except element, RELAX
    NG, 128
extends element,
    Schematron, 156
extension element, XML
    Schema, 74
external subsets, DTDs, 33
  with internal, 39
externalRef element, RELAX
    NG, 128

F

facets
  constraining, 102–117
  fundamental, 102
field element, XML Schema, 75
float element, XML Schema, 90
fractionDigits element, XML
    Schema, 104

G

gDay element, XML Schema, 91
global attributes, 51
global elements, 51
gMonth element, XML
    Schema, 91
gMonthDay element, XML
    Schema, 92
grammar element, RELAX
    NG, 130
group element, RELAX NG, 131
group element, XML
    Schema, 75
gYear element, XML Schema, 92
gYearMonth element, XML
    Schema, 93

H

hexBinary element, XML
    Schema, 93

I

ID element, XML Schema, 93
IDREF element, XML
    Schema, 94
IDREFS element, XML
    Schema, 94
import element, XML
    Schema, 76
include element, RELAX
    NG, 132
include element,
    Schematron, 156

include element, XML
        Schema, 77
int element, XML Schema, 94
integer element, XML
        Schema, 95
interleave element, RELAX
        NG, 134
internal subsets, DTDs, 37
    with external, 39

K

key element, XML Schema, 77
keyref element, XML
        Schema, 78

L

language element, XML
        Schema, 95
language, xml:space
        attribute, 28
leaf element, 11
length element, XML
        Schema, 105
let element, Schematron, 156
list element, RELAX NG, 135
list element, XML Schema, 78
long element, XML Schema, 95

M

markup, 5
maxExclusive element, XML
        Schema, 105
maxInclusive element, XML
        Schema, 106
maxLength element, XML
        Schema, 106
minExclusive element, XML
        Schema, 107
minInclusive element, XML
        Schema, 108

minLength element, XML
        Schema, 108
mixed content, 12
    DTDs, 45
    XML Schema, 61
mixed element, RELAX NG, 136
model groups, XML
        schemas, 60

N

name element, RELAX NG, 137
name element, Schematron, 157
Name element, XML
        Schema, 96
named type definitions,
        schemas, 54
namespaces, 29
    emulation, DTDs, 37
    XLink, 31
    XML Schema, 52
NCName element, XML
        Schema, 96
negativeInteger element, XML
        Schema, 96
nesting elements, 9
nil attribute, XML Schema
        instance, 117
NMTOKEN element, XML
        Schema, 97
NMTOKENS element, XML
        Schema, 97
noNamespaceSchemaLocation
        attribute, XML Schema
        instance, 117
nonNegativeInteger element,
        XML Schema, 98
nonPositiveInteger element,
        XML Schema, 98
normalizedString element, XML
        Schema, 98
notAllowed element, RELAX
        NG, 138

NOTATION element, XML
Schema, 99
notation element, XML
Schema, 79
ns element, Schematron, 157
nsName element, RELAX
NG, 139

O

oneOrMore element, RELAX
NG, 140
optional declarations, 20
optional element, RELAX
NG, 140

P

p element, Schematron, 157
param element, RELAX
NG, 141
param element,
Schematron, 158
parameter entities, 33, 43
parent element, 11
parentRef element, RELAX
NG, 143
parsed character data, 19
parsed entities
DTDs and, 41
unparsed entities, 45
pattern element,
Schematron, 153
pattern element, XML
Schema, 109
phase element, Schematron, 158
positiveInteger element, XML
Schema, 99
predefined entity references, 16
processing instructions, 4, 22
pseudo-attributes, 23

Q

QName element, XML
Schema, 99

R

redefine element, XML
Schema, 79
ref element, RELAX NG, 145
RELAX NG, 118–150
report element,
Schematron, 158
restriction element, XML
Schema, 80
rng:anyName element, 119
rng:attribute element, 120
rng:choice element, 121
rng:data element, 122
rng:define element, 123
rng:div element, 125
rng:element element, 126
rng:empty element, 127
rng:except element, 128
rng:externalRef element, 128
rng:grammar element, 130
rng:group element, 131
rng:include element, 132
rng:interleave element, 134
rng:list element, 135
rng:mixed element, 136
rng:name element, 137
rng:notAllowed element, 138
rng:nsName element, 139
rng:oneOrMore element, 140
rng:optional element, 140
rng:param element, 141
rng:parentRef element, 143
rng:ref element, 145
rng:start element, 146
rng:text element, 147
rng:value element, 148

rng:zeroOrMore element, 149
root (document) element, 10
rule element, Schematron, 153

S

sch:active element, 154
sch:assert element, 154
sch:diagnostic element, 154
sch:diagnostics element, 155
sch:dir element, 155
sch:emph element, 155
sch:extends element, 156
sch:include element, 156
sch:let element, 156
sch:name element, 157
sch:ns element, 157
sch:p element, 157
sch:param element, 158
sch:pattern element, 153
sch:phase element, 158
sch:report element, 158
sch:rule element, 153
sch:schema element, 152
sch:span element, 159
sch:title element, 159
sch:value-of element, 159
schema element,
        Schematron, 152
schema element, XML
        Schema, 80
schema, XML
    annotations, 63
    attributes, instance
        documents, 116–117
    constraining facets, 102–116
    creating, 48–64
    datatypes, 85–102
    default values, 61
    document structures, 56
    elements, 64–85
    empty content, 61
    mixed content, 61
    model groups, 60
    namespaces and, 52
    RELAX NG, 118–150
    structures, elements, 64–85
    type definitions
        anonymous, 54
        named, 54
    WXS (W3C SML Schema), 47
    XSD (XML schema), 47
schemaLocation attribute, XML
        Schema instance, 117
Schematron, 150–159
    core elements, 152
sections, conditional, DTDs, 45
selector element, XML
        Schema, 82
sequence element, XML
        Schema, 82
SGML (Standard Generalized
        Markup Language), 2
short element, XML
        Schema, 100
sibling elements, 11
simpleContent element, XML
        Schema, 83
simpleType element, XML
        Schema, 83
span element, Schematron, 159
specifications listing, 160
standalone document
        declarations, 22
start element, RELAX NG, 146
start-tags, 8
string element, XML
        Schema, 100
structures, 5
    attributes, 13
        elements, 14
    CDATA sections, 24
    character references, 16
    comments, 19
    DOCTYPE declaration, 24

elements, 6–13
  ancestor elements, 11
  attributes and, 14
  child element, 11
  descendant element, 11
  leaf element, 11
  parent element, 11
  schemas, 64–85
  sibling elements, 11
entity references, 16
mixed content, 12
namespaces, 29
predefined entity
  references, 16
processing instructions, 22
root (document) element, 10
schema, XML, 56
text, 15
  characters, 15
  whitespace, 16
XML declarations, 20
xml:id attribute, 28
xml:lang attribute, 27
xml:space attribute, 26
system identifiers, 34

T

tags
  empty-element tags, 9
  end-tags, 8
  start-tags, 8
targets, processing
  instructions, 23
text, 15
  characters, 15
  whitespace, 16
text declaration, DTDs, 35
text element, RELAX NG, 147
time element, XML Schema, 100
title element, Schematron, 159
token element, XML
  Schema, 101

totalDigits element, XML
  Schema, 115
type attribute, XML Schema
  instance, 117
type definitions, XML Schema
  anonymous, 54
  named, 54

U

union element, XML
  Schema, 84
unique element, XML
  Schema, 84
unparsed entities, DTDs, 45
unsignedByte element, XML
  Schema, 101
unsignedInt element, XML
  Schema, 101
unsignedLong element, XML
  Schema, 102
unsignedShort element, XML
  Schema, 102

V

value element, RELAX NG, 148
value-of element,
  Schematron, 159

W

well-formed documents, 3
whitespace, 16
  xml:space attribute, 26
whiteSpace element, XML
  Schema, 115
WXS (W3C XML Schema), 47

X

XLink (XML Linking
  Language), 31
XML declarations, 20

XML Schema
  constraining facets, 102–116
  creating, 48–64
  datatypes, 85–102
  default values, 61
  document structures, 56
  elements, 64–85
  empty content, 61
  instance documents, 116–117
  mixed content, 61
  model groups, 60
  namespaces, 52
  RELAX NG, 118–150
  structures, 64–85
  structures, elements, 64–85
  type definitions
    anonymous, 54
    named, 54
  WXS (W3C SML Schema), 47
  XSD (XML schema), 47
xml:id attribute, 28
xml:lang attribute, 27
xml:space attribute, 26
XSD (XML Schema), 47
xs:all element, 64
xs:annotation element, 65
xs:any element, 65
xs:anyAttribute element, 66
xs:anySimpleType element, 85
xs:anyURL element, 85
xs:appInfo element, 67
xs:attribute element, 67
xs:attributeGroup element, 69
xs:base64binary element, 86
xs:boolean element, 86
xs:byte element, 87
xs:choice element, 69
xs:complexContent element, 70
xs:complexType element, 70
xs:date element, 87
xs:dateTime element, 87
xs:decimal element, 88
xs:documentation element, 72

xs:double element, 88
xs:duration element, 89
xs:element element, 72
xs:ENTITIES element, 90
xs:ENTITY element, 90
xs:enumeration element, 103
xs:extension element, 74
xs:field element, 75
xs:float element, 90
xs:fractionDigits element, 104
xs:gDay element, 91
xs:gMonth element, 91
xs:gMonthDay element, 92
xs:group element, 75
xs:gYear element, 92
xs:gYearMonth element, 93
xs:hexBinary element, 93
xs:ID element, 93
xs:IDREF element, 94
xs:IDREFS element, 94
xs:import element, 76
xs:include element, 77
xs:int element, 94
xs:integer element, 95
xs:key element, 77
xs:keyref element, 78
xs:language element, 95
xs:length element, 105
xs:list element, 78
xs:long element, 95
xs:maxExclusive element, 105
xs:maxInclusive element, 106
xs:maxLength element, 106
xs:minExclusive element, 107
xs:minInclusive element, 108
xs:minLength element, 108
xs:Name element, 96
xs:NCName element, 96
xs:negativeInteger element, 96
xs:NMTOKEN element, 97
xs:NMTOKENS element, 97
xs:nonNegativeInteger, 98

xs:nonPositiveInteger
    element, 98
xs:normalizedString element, 98
xs:NOTATION element, 99
xs:notation element, 79
xs:pattern element, 109
xs:positiveInteger element, 99
xs:QName element, 99
xs:redefine element, 79
xs:restriction element, 80
xs:schema element, 80
xs:selector element, 82
xs:sequence element, 82
xs:short element, 100
xs:simpleContent element, 83
xs:simpleType element, 83
xs:string element, 100
xs:time element, 100
xs:token element, 101

xs:totalDigits element, 115
xs:union element, 84
xs:unique element, 84
xs:unsignedByte element, 101
xs:unsignedInt element, 101
xs:unsignedLong element, 102
xs:unsignedShort element, 102
xs:whiteSpace element, 115
xsi:nil attribute, 117
xsi:noNamespaceSchema-
    Location attribute, 117
xsi:schemaLocation
    attribute, 117
xsi:type attribute, 117

Z

zeroOrMore element, RELAX
    NG, 149